Christmas
in Mexico

Christmas in Mexico

¡Feliz Navidad! ¡Feliz Navidad! ¡Feliz Navidad! ¡Feliz Navidad! ¡Feliz Navidad! ¡Feliz Navidad! ¡Feliz Navidad! ¡Feliz Navidad! ¡Feliz Navidad! ¡Feliz Navidad! ¡Feliz Navidad! ¡Feliz Navidad!

Corinne Ross

PASSPORT BOOKS
a division of *NTC Publishing Group*
Lincolnwood, Illinois USA

1994 Printing

This edition first published in 1991 by Passport Books, a division of NTC Publishing Group,
4255 West Touhy Avenue, Lincolnwood (Chicago), Illinois 60646-1975 U.S.A.
© 1976 by World Book, Inc. All rights reserved. No part
of this book may be reproduced, stored in a retrieval
system, or transmitted in any form, or by any means,
electronic, mechanical, photocopying or otherwise,
without the prior permission of NTC Publishing Group.
Manufactured in Hong Kong.

3 4 5 6 7 8 9 LR 9 8 7 6 5 4

Contents

Map of Mexico

Showing the location of the places mentioned in this book.

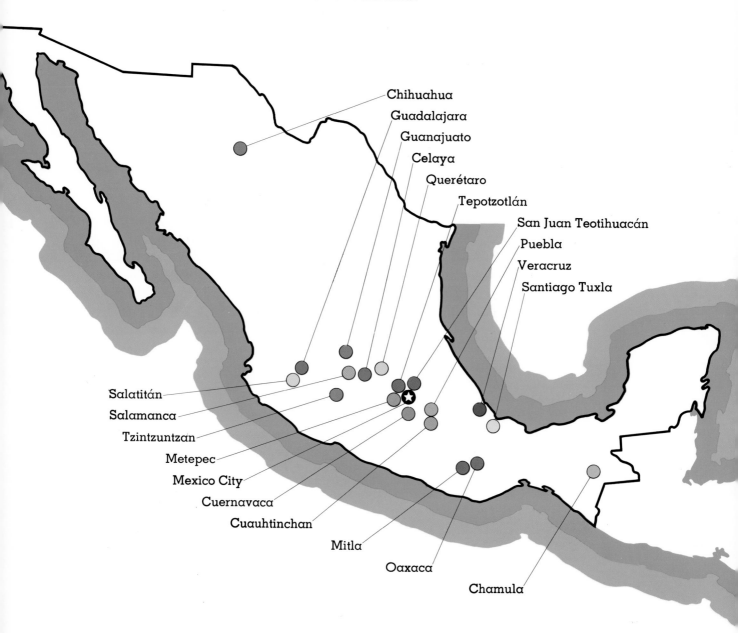

Chihuahua

Guadalajara

Guanajuato

Celaya

Querétaro

Tepotzotlán

San Juan Teotihuacán

Puebla

Veracruz

Santiago Tuxla

Salatitán

Salamanca

Tzintzuntzan

Metepec

Mexico City

Cuernavaca

Cuauhtinchan

Mitla

Oaxaca

Chamula

Pronunciation glossary

Inevitably, this book contains many foreign words.
They are listed below together with their respelled pronunciations.
The accented syllable appears in small capital letters.

aguinaldo
ah gee NAHL doh

arbol de la vida
AHR bohl deh lah
VEE dah

atole
ah TOH leh

Bamba
BAHM bah

Belenes
beh LEH nehs

buñuelo
boo NYWEH loh

Caimán
kahy MAHN

calendas
cah LEHN dahs

capirotada
kah pee roh TAH dah

casas de vecindad
CAH sahs deh
veh seen DAH

castillo
cahs TEE yoh

Celaya
seh LAH yah

champurrado
chahm poo RRAH doh

Chamula
chah MOO lah

charros
CHAH rros

Chichimecas
chee chee MEH kahs

chinas
CHEE nahs

chocolatl
choh koh LAHT'l

Coatlicue
koh aht LEE kweh

colaciones
koh lah SYOH nehs

comadre
koh MAH dreh

cuetlaxóchitl
kweh tlah SOH cheet'l

Día de la Candelaria
DEE yah deh lah
kahn deh LAH ryah

Día de los Inocentes
DEE yah deh lohs
ee noh SEHN tehs

Día de los Reyes
DEE yah deh lohs
REH yehs

empanadas
ehm pah NAH dahs

faroles
fah ROH lehs

Feliz Año Nuevo
feh LEES AH nyoh
NWEH voh

Flor de la Noche Buena
flohr deh lah
NOH cheh BWEH nah

glorietas
gloh RYEH tahs

Guadalajara
gwah dah lah HAH rah

Guanajuato
gwah nah HWAH toh

huapango
wah PAHN goh

Huitzilopochtli
wee tsee loh POHCH tlee

lama
LAH mah

matachines
mah tah CHEE nehs

Metepec
meh teh PEHK

Michoacán
mee choh ah KAHN

Misa de Gallo
MEE sah deh GAH yoh

misterios
mees TEH ryohs

Mitla
MEET lah

mole
MOH leh

Montezuma
mohn teh soo mah

Moros y Cristianos
MOH rohs ee
krees TYAH nohs

nacimiento
nah see MYEHN toh

Nahuatl
NAH waht'l

Navidad
nah vee DAH

Noche Buena
NOH cheh BWEH nah

Noche de los Rábanos
NOH cheh deh lohs
RAH bah nohs

Oaxaca
wah HAH kah

olla
OH yah

Panduro
pahn DOO roh

Pascuas
PAHS kwahs

pastorelas
pahs toh REH lahs

pastores
pahs TOH rehs

Pedido de la Cruz
peh DEE doh deh lah
kroos

pignatta
pee NYAHT tah

piñata
pee NYAH tah

posadas
poh SAH dahs

pozole
poh SOH leh

Querétaro
keh REH tah roh

Rama
RAH mah

Rosca de Reyes
ROHS kah deh REH yehs

Salamanca
sah lah MAHN kah

Santiago Matamoros
sahn TYAH goh
mah tah MOH rohs

Santiago Tuxla
sahn TYAH goh
TOOSK lah

Sembradoras
sehm brah DOH rahs

Sociedad Folklórica
soh syeh DAH
fohl KLOH ree kah

tejocotes
teh hoh KOH tehs

Tepotzotlán
teh poh soh TLAHN

Torito
toh REE toh

torrejas de coco
toh RREH hahs deh
KOH koh

Tzintzuntzan
tseen TSOON tsahn

Veracruz
veh rah KROOS

Viejitos
vyeh HEE tohs

Xala
SAH lah

Zócalo
SOH kah loh

zumpantle
soom PAHN tleh

7

Introduction

Scarlet poinsettias, frilly piñatas and gay clusters of balloons, religious banners, images of saints, candlelit processions and comic theatricals—they're all part of the exciting pageant that is Christmastime in Mexico. The holiday season is a swirling kaleidoscope of riotous color and gaiety, a joyous fiesta that lasts for weeks.

Many Mexicans take a vacation at this time of year, and schoolchildren have an extra-long holiday. Thousands of people swarm to the beaches; others choose the mountains or join in the festivities that are taking place in every village, town, and city throughout the land. It's a time of togetherness, too, when families and friends gather—to visit and share in the celebrations.

The climate is ideal for every kind of activity—the days warm and sunny, the nights cool and refreshing. Brilliant masses of flowers scent the air and the lively music of Mexico brightens spirits even more. Towering coconut palms and bougainvillea-covered patio walls, gurgling fountains and red-tiled roofs present an exotic sight to travelers accustomed to the icy slush and cold of northern winters. Fascinating markets invite exploring, shopwindows and lavish displays attract the eye; all around, there's an endless array of exciting things to do and see.

The holidays begin on December 16th, when the nine-day *posada* processions start and the nativity scenes called *nacimientos* are set up in every home and public square. On Christmas Eve, after the last posada is over, everyone goes to a solemn midnight Mass, and Christmas Day is welcomed in with a jubilant medley of bells, whistles, and firecrackers.

The festivities continue with the Day of the Innocents on December 28th, New Year's Eve on the 31st, and the Day of the Three Kings on January 6th. One final celebration on February 2nd—Candlemas—winds up the season.

Every region of Mexico celebrates Christmas in its own distinctive way—with traditional dances and plays, bullfights, rodeos, parades and special holiday foods. The Christmas observances of today are a piquant blend of Spanish and Indian cultures, a commingling of old customs and new variations . . . with roots that go back more than four hundred years.

The Epiphany, a 17th-century
oil painting by the Mexican
artist José Juarez.

How it all began

The mighty civilizations of the Mayas, Toltecs, Chichimecas, and, finally, the Aztecs ruled Mexico in their turn. Spanish explorers discovered this strange new world in the 16th century. In 1519, Hernan Cortés led an expeditionary army to conquer the Aztec empire—and capture its fantastic treasury of gold. Sixteen years later, Mexico became a Spanish colony, which it remained until 1821.

With the conquistadores came Catholic missionaries, bringing their Christian faith to the pagan land. By a strange coincidence, the Aztecs celebrated the birth of their god Huitzilopochtli during the last days of December, around the winter solstice, at about the same time as Christmas.

According to legend, Huitzilopochtli's mother, Coatlicue, was struck by a plumed ball of feathers while she was sweeping the steps of the temple, and in due course gave birth to the new god. Her other sons refused to believe the story of the supernatural conception and decided to kill her, but Huitzilopochtli appeared, armed with a fire serpent, and destroyed his scheming brothers.

The festival celebrating Huitzilopochtli's birth was the most important one of the Aztec year. It began at midnight and continued through the following day, with much singing, dancing, and speechmaking. The Indians paraded under elaborate arches of roses, wearing their finest attire adorned with brightly tinted plumes. Special foods were prepared, including small idols made of corn paste and cactus honey, and huge bonfires in courtyards and on the flat roofs of the houses lit up the sky for miles around.

The missionaries, noting the similarities between their own commemoration of the birth of Christ and the Aztecs' December observances, found it a relatively simple matter to substitute a new faith for the old. The ancient god of war with his cruel tradition of blood sacrifices was replaced by a gentle one of love and hope, represented by a tiny babe, the Christ Child.

The first Christmas in old Mexico was celebrated in 1538 by Fray Pedro de Gante. He invited all the Indians for twenty leagues around Mexico City to attend, and they came in droves, some by land, others by water. Even the sick managed to come, carried in hammocks. The Indians loved the new feast day, and adopted it wholeheartedly, adding their own colorful touches of flowers and feathers.

So many assembled for the Christmas Masses that they spilled over into the courtyard of the church and caused such a jam that those in front were in danger of being smothered. Those outside followed the ritual just as attentively as the ones indoors, however, and one padre later related that the natives would not

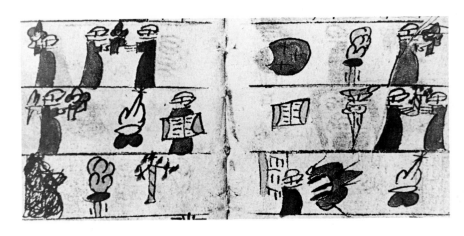

Simple stories of Jesus' life are shown in this catechism drawn in 1528 by the Spanish missionary, Fray Pedro de Gante.

The Adoration of the Shepherds,
a 17th-century Mexican oil
painting by Pedro Ramirez.

miss a midnight Mass for anything in the world.

The numbers of enthusiastic new churchgoers continued to grow over the years. In 1587, Fray Diego de Soria, prior of the Convent of San Agustín Acolman, tried to alleviate the overcrowded situation. He asked the Pope in Rome for permission to hold the Christmas Masses out-of-doors in the church courtyard. It was given, and the services—held from December 16th to the 24th— were called *Misas de Aquinaldo*.

Many of Mexico's present-day Christmas traditions were originally introduced during the colonial era as a means of teaching Christian morals and the Bible to the Indians. The *posadas*, a nine-night series of processions reenacting Joseph and Mary's journey to Bethlehem, began in this way. Medieval European passion plays were adapted by the missionaries for the natives, and sometimes even translated into Nahuatl, the Aztec language. These developed into the Christmas dramas called *pastorelas*. The 16th-century priests also brought the custom of smashing a gaily decorated pot called the piñata to the New World, using it as a finale to the Christmas Masses.

Religious paintings and sculpture brought to Mexico in the 1500's very often portrayed scenes of the Nativity and other Biblical events. The Indians greatly admired these works and eventually began to create their own interpretations of the old scenes. The Virgin Mary's face took on a darker hue; bone structure—and dress—became more and more Indian in appearance.

The custom of erecting a Christmas manger scene, called a *nacimiento*, was probably not introduced in the New World until a bit later, in the 1700's. In any case, the small nacimiento figures, originally European in feature and dress, quickly developed their own native characteristics, too.

In time, many of the rites once

This 16th-century polychromed and gilded wood sculpture attributed to Juan de Arrúe, represents St. Ann, the Virgin Mary, and Jesus.

Posada, a mural by the famous Mexican artist Diego Rivera in the Children's Hospital in Mexico City.

In this woodcut depicting a colonial posada, children carrying candles are followed by friends and relatives, a guitar-playing musician, and a family pet.

held in the churches moved to people's homes and into the public squares. By the middle of the 1600's, images and paintings of the Virgin Mary or the Three Kings could be seen in the windows of almost every house during the holiday season. Lights shone from every window, and balconies were illuminated with candles, protected from the wind by glass bells. Some homeowners erected magnificent altars in front of their houses and hung gorgeous rugs and tapestries from the balconies. The rosary was recited aloud in the streets. People met and mingled in the main squares, enjoying the decorations and visiting busy market stalls.

The Indians' habit of enlivening the solemn Spanish religious observances with their own gregarious practices occasionally dismayed the priests. In 1796, the Archbishop of Mexico complained that there was so much noise during the Aguinaldo

Masses—including whistles, rattles, and tambourines—and so much munching on fruit and sweets, that all respect for the holy observances themselves was being lost. Even worse, in later years all sorts of nonreligious songs began to sneak into the Christmas Masses.

During the colonial era, Mexico was ruled by viceroys, or governors appointed by the king. The day before Christmas the viceroy, accompanied by his court, would make the rounds of prisons and free prisoners convicted of minor offenses. The vicereine, his wife, would feed and clothe groups of impoverished children. Lavish parties were given in the viceregal palace, attended by all the upper-class society folk, with parlor games (card games were strictly forbidden), music, and refreshments. All of these persons of distinction also visited the cathedral to hear lengthy sermons; a proper sermon in those days could easily last an hour, and often began with the Creation, to make sure that everything important was covered.

One custom of the early 19th century resembled Halloween trick-or-treating. In the days preceding Christmas, bands of children carrying a small manger scene would roam the streets, stopping at every house or shop to sing and ask for treats. The pleas were ingeniously pathetic: "My mule got lost and I am heartbroken, because she was carrying a gift for the Christ Child." Only hearts of iron would refuse to contribute to another gift for the newborn babe . . . or perhaps the besieged householder or shopkeeper merely wished to prevent mischievous pranks.

In the adult version of this custom, the lamplighter, street cleaner, water carrier, garbageman, or postman would come around with little printed cards offering good wishes for the coming year. In return, they would receive a Christmas gift. This custom, like so many others dating back to colonial times, still continues today in many parts of Mexico.

15

Nativity scenes, called nacimientos, have become a uniquely
Mexican art form. This cardboard
nacimiento is painted in what is
known as Mexican pink.

Nacimientos

Christmas in Mexico is called la Navidad . . . the nativity. And even though the holiday season there is an extraordinarily festive time, the true religious meaning of the celebration is not forgotten. Each year on December 16th, nacimientos, miniature representations of the birth of Christ, are set up in homes throughout the country, in great cities, small towns, and villages. Nacimientos are also displayed in churches, store windows, government and business buildings, and in plazas and public parks, where they become gathering places for Christmas choral programs.

In some parts of the world this endearing Biblical re-creation is called a crèche, or manger scene. Whatever its name, the tableau always includes a stable, and figures of Mary, Joseph, and the Christ Child. Its theme is the story of that wondrous night in Bethlehem—almost 2,000 years ago.

In Mexico, the nacimiento takes on a rainbow of national and individual characteristics. It becomes just about anything its creators want it to be, from a simple grouping of the Holy Family to the entire countryside of Bethlehem populated by a diversity of people and animals, the whole bedecked with fresh blossoms and Spanish moss.

Perhaps the most delightful aspect of the south-of-the-border manger scene is its total incongruity—a donkey may be larger than the stable, the setting may include a Noah's Ark or Herod's palace, and the Three Kings may be dressed in the style of long-ago Spanish grandees while Joseph and Mary appear in contemporary garb. The centuries-old Bethlehem scene will most likely include distinctively Mexican characters such as a taco seller, balloon vendor, village beauty, or water carrier. Anachronistic bells may appear in the temple of Solomon, or Louis XV chairs and chaise longues of the time of Josephine in the Virgin's house; hermits dressed in Franciscan habits may be seen kneeling in worship before a crucifix in a cave. Even the weather portrayed is a mishmash of geographical confusion: luxuriant tropical flowers mix unconcernedly with frosty imitation snow.

Biblical history is presented in some unorthodox ways, too: Jesus may be observed among the wise men of the Temple, or performing the miracle of the fishes and loaves, and the baptism in the River Jordan or even the Slaughter of the Innocents could well be included. Adam and Eve, Cain and Abel, Joseph about to be sold by his brothers—all manner of Biblical characters somehow find their places, albeit out of chronological whack, conjoining the humble trio of the original Nativity.

The custom of erecting a manger scene can be traced far back in history . . . to, it is thought, St. Francis of Assisi. In 1223, he supposedly journeyed to the Convent of Monte Columbo. Upon reaching it, the gentle saint told a friend that he wanted to celebrate Christmas by creating a Nativity scene, with a live donkey and an ox, as a reminder of Christ's humble birth.

From Italy, the custom traveled to Spain, probably first appearing there in the 17th century. The earliest manger scenes in Mexico —in the 18th century—were most likely derived from the famed Spanish *belenes*, which were exhibited not only to churches, but also in the palaces of the grandees. Soon every household in Mexico, rich or poor, had its own nacimiento at Christmastime.

At first, they generally included only the three main figures of Joseph, Mary, and Jesus, and were called *misterios* (mysteries). The central part of all nacimientos today is still referred to

In this elaborate nacimiento (right) from a private home in Oaxaca, ceramic angels guard the Christ Child in the grotto. Glittering with jewels, the opulently clothed Three Kings (below) bring gifts to the Christ Child.

by that name. In time, other figures began to be added, usually carved in wood and painted, the faces and hands sometimes made of wax. Zumpantle, a wood as light as cork and therefore easy to carve, was extensively used. The sculptures were covered with a thin coat of plaster and then painted with brilliant colors, often over a first coat of silver or gold. Beautiful costumes for the figures were sewn by nuns in the convents or by the daughters of the house.

Manger groupings were once considered highly valuable property. An inventory of household goods left upon the death of the Countess of Xala in 1788 lists 117 figures of the Magi and their entourage, six princes in cloth garments and silver ornaments, 112 shepherdesses and 18 shepherds, an angel, several Indians, an ox and a mule, 34 sheep of different sizes, 16 cows, an old man leading a horse, 36 small animals, a hut with an old woman feeding her chickens, four small houses, and a whole grove of trees. The estimated value of the set was $1,077, a fortune for that time.

The 18th century was a flourishing one for the art of nacimientos; the most talented artists collabo-

Flat, brightly painted figures of Joseph, Mary, and Baby Jesus (*left*) are surrounded by three-dimensional ornaments in this colorful manger scene. Ceramic figures of the Holy Family, Wise Men, and villagers dot a nacimiento landscape (*lower left*). Straw figures, stable, and star (*bottom left*) make up this simple Nativity setting.

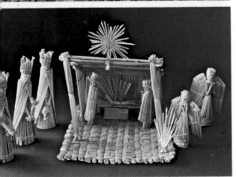

rated in their production, and the colors were remarkably vivid. Some of the central figures were brought from Guatemala, then famous for its multicolored manger pieces. With the rise of the mining industry in Mexico, many figures began to be made of precious silver. Porcelain pieces were imported from Italy, and ivory ones from China or the Philippines.

In the latter half of the 19th century, the custom—and quality —of nacimientos went into a decline, especially in Mexico City. That was a time when traditional values were being questioned during the revolutionary turmoil that followed the war for independence. This decline continued into the present century, partly due to the wide adoption of certain northern Yuletide symbols, such as Santa Claus and the Christmas tree. But in recent years a resurgence of interest has sprung up, along with an increased consciousness of the true value of native Mexican art and customs, and the nacimiento has once again become an integral part of the Mexican Christmas.

On the 16th of December or even earlier in the month, the tucked-away boxes of nacimiento figures are brought out. Each piece is checked for any damage that might have occurred during the year, and new additions will be purchased at the market if needed. Creating the scene is a lengthy process, and the whole family gets involved. The nacimiento will be set up on a table or in the corner of a room—occasionally an especially grandiose nativity scene will take up the entire room.

A wooden base slants upwards, representing hills or mountains; hay sometimes pads out the slopes. Moss and artificial grass provide lush greenery, bits of pine, the foliage. Typically, a long winding road of white sand goes from the top of the mountain all the way down to the valley. There may be a river or lake made of pieces of mirror or tinfoil, and small huts are set alongside the road. Inappropriate though it may be, there must be snow . . . made of cotton or talcum powder. Flowers bank the hillsides, white cotton clouds are glued to a blue backdrop, and above it all, the star of Bethlehem shines down.

Finally, the figures are added to the scene . . . pilgrims march along the roadway toward the stable far below. Shepherds and the Three Kings approach on smaller paths, and here and there are flocks of sheep, grazing hap-

The town of Metepec is renowned for a unique creation of
polychromed ceramic called
Arbol de la Vida or *Tree of Life*.
The special Christmas *Tree of
Life* (right) has a Nativity
scene in the center.

pily on the winter-summer landscape, watched over by other
shepherds and their dogs.

An array of villagers is
grouped in the vicinity of the
stable—the village fool, washer-
women, fishermen, all sorts of
everyday people going about
their everyday tasks. An angel or
two hovers nearby, watching
over the Holy Family. Then there
are the animals. Horses, donkeys,
dogs, camels, chickens, goats,
turkeys—but never a pig. Pigs
are not native to ancient Judea.
Never mind that turkeys aren't,
either—that's one more of those
delightful incongruities. There
may even be an electric train
buzzing along on tiny tracks, or a
jet plane swooshing overhead.
Close by, as often as not, a
Christmas tree imported from
Canada will spread its boughs
over the scene.

Each region of Mexico special-
izes in different types of manger
characters. The state of Guanajuato is renowned for its won-
drously detailed nacimientos—
especially in Celaya and Salamanca. These elaborate scenes
include tiny fountains and
streams of real water; live ferns
and orchids grow among the
rocks, and flying angels cast their
blessings on the figures below.

The gifted Panduro family of
Guadalajara produces outstand-
ingly beautiful manger scenes
with intriguingly realistic folk figures. In Mexico City, the famous
poet Carlos Pellicer makes his
own wax figures and each year
re-creates different geographical
areas of Mexico, meticulously
collecting the correct indigenous
plants and rocks of the region.
From Metepec, Mexico, comes the
intricate, colorfully painted, clay
"tree of life," with its representations of the Virgin and Child,
Adam and Eve, God, the sun and
moon, animals of all kinds, and
generations of Biblical families—
a novel variation of the traditional Nativity scene.

Nacimiento figures may be
made of glass, silver, lead, porcelain—even cardboard or plastic.
Tiny figures of wheat straw, dried
flowers, clay, or wood may be
left unadorned or are ornamented
with marvelous designs. Nacimientos may include ladies with
prehispanic headdresses, devils
instead of angels, fantastic animals, and an eccentric selection
of mixed-up Bible characters
ranged in happy proximity alongside homely ranks of native village types—there is seemingly no
end to the prodigious variety and
engaging inventiveness of the
Mexican Nativity scenes.

Throngs of children and adults
gather for a Christmas Eve
posada in Oaxaca. Their paper
lanterns give the town an
eerie glow.

Posadas

Posadas tend to be festive and joyous affairs, but this girl (*left*) from the village of Xoxo approaches the event full of solemn devotion.

"And it came to pass in those days, that there went out a decree from Caesar Augustus, that all the world should be taxed. And all went to be taxed, every one into his own city. And Joseph also went up from Galilee, out of the city of Nazareth, into Judea, unto the city of David, which is called Bethlehem (because he was of the house and lineage of David), to be taxed with Mary his espoused wife, being great with child."

"And so it was, that while they were there, the days were accomplished that she should be delivered. And she brought forth her firstborn son, and wrapped him in swaddling clothes and laid him in a manger, because there was no room for them in the inn.'"

Luke 2:1–7

This familiar Bible story is related every year at Christmastime in churches and homes the world over. In Mexico each December, it actually comes to life once again, as Joseph and Mary's long-ago search for lodgings is reenacted for nine consecutive nights in the festive ritual of *las posadas*. "Posada" means inn, or lodging, in Spanish.

The idea of commemorating the holy family's journey to Bethlehem can be traced back to St. Ignatius Loyola, in the 16th century. He suggested a Christmas novena, or special prayers to be said on nine successive days. In 1580, St. John of the Cross made a religious pageant out of the proceedings, and seven years later the nine-day remembrance was introduced to the Indians in Mexico by Spanish missionaries.

Solemn and deeply religious in feeling at first, the observances soon became imbued with a spirit of fun and, eventually, left the church and began to be celebrated in people's homes. The posadas have become a community affair with friends, relatives, and neighbors getting together to share in the festivities, visiting a different house each evening.

The posada begins with a procession that sets off as soon as it gets dark. Usually a child dressed as an angel heads the procession, followed by two more children carrying figures of Mary and Joseph on a small litter adorned with twigs of pine. Groups of boys and girls follow the lead figures, then come the grown-ups, and last of all, the musicians. Singing or chanting special posada songs, they all walk slowly along, each person carrying a lighted candle, the children tootling on shrill whistles. When the procession reaches the house chosen for that evening, it divides into two groups, one representing the holy pilgrims, the other the innkeepers.

The pilgrims line up behind the angel and the children bearing

An ancient church is the starting-off place for a Christmas *posada* procession in Oaxaca. Singing traditional litanies, the marchers act out the Holy Family's search for shelter in long-ago Bethlehem, ending the evening with a festive party.

the figures of the Holy Family, and they file through the house until they arrive at a closed door, behind which the innkeepers have stationed themselves. The pilgrims knock on the door and call out in song, asking for shelter. A chorus of voices on the other side asks: "Who knocks at my door so late in the night?"

The pilgrims respond, "In the name of Heaven I beg you for lodging—my beloved wife can no longer travel, and she is weary." But the response is a stony, hardhearted refusal. "This is no inn. Go away!" After repeated requests for shelter, the pilgrims explain who they are, and that Mary will soon give birth to the Son of God. The innkeepers relent and welcome the exhausted travelers: "Enter, holy pilgrims. Come into our humble dwelling and into our hearts. The night is one of joy, for here beneath our roof we shelter the Mother of God."

Everyone enters the room and kneels in prayer, after which the party moves out to the patio for fireworks and fun. Small baskets of sweets, called *colaciones*, are offered along with sandwiches, cookies, and a fruited punch—and then it's time for the most exciting moment of all—the breaking of the fancifully deco-

A small boy with a wide grin and a paper lantern with a candle inside are all set to illuminate a *calenda* procession in Oaxaca.

rated, candy- and nut-filled piñata. Sometimes there are separate parties for different age groups—one for teen-agers, and another for the younger children. In Mexico City, especially, so many posadas are held that active partygoers can manage to attend four or five in one evening . . . and the festivities often go on until dawn.

For eight nights virtually the same ceremonies are repeated. But on the ninth evening, Christmas Eve, a particularly impressive posada takes place, during which an image of the Christ Child is carried in by two people who are called the godparents, and laid in His tiny crib in the nacimiento.

Frances Calderón de la Barca, a Scotswoman married to a Spanish diplomat, traveled extensively in Mexico in the mid-1800's. In her book, *Life in Mexico*, she described a Christmas Eve spent at the house of a noble lady of that day:

"This is the last night of what are called the *Posadas*, a curious mixture of religion and amusement, but extremely pretty. We went to the Marquesa's at eight o'clock, and about nine the ceremony commenced. A lighted taper is put into the hand of each lady, and a procession was

Carefully carrying an image of the Baby Jesus, a young girl walks toward the manger, paper lanterns lighting her way. It is the end of a Christmas Eve posada in a private home, the moment when the Christ Child is placed in his crib in the nacimiento.

formed, which marched all through the house, the corridors and walls of which were all decorated with evergreens and lamps, the whole party singing the Litanies. A group of little children joined the procession. They wore little robes of silver or gold *lama*, plumes of white feathers, and a profusion of fine diamonds and pearls, in bandeaus, brooches, and necklaces, white gauze wings, and white satin shoes, embroidered in gold.

"At last the procession drew up before a door, and a shower of fireworks was sent flying over our heads, I suppose to represent the descent of the angels—for a group of ladies appeared, dressed to represent the shepherds who watched their flocks at night upon the plains of Bethlehem. Voices, supposed to be those of Mary and Joseph, struck up a hymn, in which they begged for admittance. . . . A chorus of voices from within refused . . . (finally) the doors were thrown open and the Holy Family entered singing.

"The scene inside was very pretty: a nacimiento. Platforms, going all around the room, were covered with moss, on top of which reposed wax figures repre-

senting parts of the New Testament. There were green trees and fruit trees, and little fountains that cast up fairy columns of water, and flocks of sheep, and a little cradle in which to lay the Infant Christ. One of the angels held a waxen baby in her arms. A padre took the baby and placed it in the cradle, and the posada was completed. We then returned to the drawing-room—angels, shepherds, and all, and danced till suppertime . . . a show for sweetmeats and cakes."

In Mexican cities today, posadas often take place in the *casas de vecindad*, tenement houses, where the rooms all open onto one big patio or courtyard. The neighbors contribute their share of the expenses, and celebrate together. In towns and villages, the posada may start in the church courtyard, wander through the streets and end up back at the church, and the piñata will often be strung up in the village square. Sometimes a Christmas Eve posada will have live people enacting the roles of the Holy Family, with Mary riding a donkey, and the procession concluding at a manger scene set up in a field.

The children carry *faroles*, transparent paper lanterns con-

taining lighted candles, attached to long poles. When the posada procession reaches the nacimiento, the youngsters offer small gifts of flowers or fruit, and each makes a little speech to the Infant Jesus. Young men portraying shepherds then appear, leading sheep and goats. One by one each man, with the help of a friend, lifts an animal onto his shoulders. Forming a circle, they dance while onlookers clap in rhythm and children toss firecrackers at their feet. In another part of the field, women prepare tamales and whip hot chocolate into foam with twirling wooden sticks, getting ready for the feasting that follows.

A truly Mexican Christmas observance, the posadas have, however, wandered north into the United States, too. San Diego, California, presents posadas at the Mission of San Luis Rey, in the Old Town section, and in the Padua Hills where performances have been given for many years. *La Sociedad Folklórica* continues the tradition in Santa Fe, and Mexican-Americans in both San Antonio, Texas, and Chicago, hold the processions annually.

Performances of pastorelas are often preceded by a procession composed of both actors and the public. Here are Mary and Joseph as they will appear in the play at Tepotzotlán.

Pastorelas

The devil is not ordinarily associated with Christmas. In Mexico, however, Lucifer plays a very solid role in the holiday festivities. He is actually the star in a special kind of drama called *pastorela*.

Usually performed in the afternoons or early evenings of the last weeks of December, pastorelas are a Mexican version of Europe's medieval miracle plays. They are most often presented outdoors—in a public square, in the courtyard of a church or inn, or in the patio of someone's home. The players may be local townsfolk, groups of schoolchildren, or semiprofessional troupes of actors who travel to different villages putting on a show every night during the Christmas season.

The performance may last from half an hour to several hours to all night—one, in the mountains of Guanajuato, goes on for two or three days. That production, with 22 actors, begins with the story of Adam and Eve and ends with the birth of Christ. Tepotzotlán, a town near Mexico City, is the scene of Mexico's most famous pastorela, performed each year from December 15th to the 23rd. Throughout the country variations abound, each community giving its own peculiar twist to the presentation.

Pastorela means pastoral, or a play that takes place in the countryside, and concerns the activities of *pastores*, or shepherds. First introduced in Mexico by missionaries in the 1500's, the pastorelas continued to grow in favor among the people, and today are one of the most popular Christmastime entertainments.

A mixture of religious teachings, Indian-Mexican folklore and ribald comedy, with the emphasis on the last, the pastorelas all tell pretty much the same story. In brief, the theme portrays the eternal conflict between good and evil. The plot revolves around the pilgrimage of the shepherds to Bethlehem to see the newborn Christ Child.

In the Bible story, they made it without any problems. In the pastorelas, however, the shepherds encounter a whole series of setbacks, all brought about by Lucifer, the Devil. Hard as he tries to disrupt their journey though, he fails every time. The drama ends in Bethlehem with the shepherds offering their humble gifts to the Infant Jesus.

Most pastorelas were handed down from generation to generation by word of mouth, as few people in the old days were literate. Because of this oral tradition, considerable changes have come about in both words and action, and new twists are constantly being added, depending on the inclination of the performers.

In the 1800's, an observer of a Christmas pastorela described how the actors met for weeks ahead of time to listen to the one man who knew the lines. He repeated them over and over until every man, woman, and child could recite their roles almost mechanically.

The few written pastorelas are always zealously guarded, for good reason. Possession of a written record allows the owner to demand the role of the director. Church libraries and town halls sometimes have copies, too.

In smaller towns, especially, the pastorelas are looked forward to with great excitement. On the night of the performance, the audience begins to straggle in early, often carrying their own chairs to sit on. The temptation to enter into the proceedings is overwhelming . . . bad guys are hissed and booed, the heroes cheered and applauded.

Combining song and poetry, imaginative costuming, dancing, and a great deal of hammy acting, pastorelas are a truly unique form of theater. Just as they did

Painted flames form a hellish backdrop as a shepherd in the famous pastorelas of Tepotzlán tells his friends about a dream of temptation sent by the Devil.

Ornate costumes and feathered headdresses highlight a pastorela procession at the Convent of Tepotzlán, near Mexico City (*below*).

with other customs introduced by the Spanish missionaries, the Mexican people added their own brand of spice to the pastorelas. Revelry in religious matters was not looked upon with too much favor by the priests, and at one time the pastorelas were banned from the church altogether. Which didn't bother the Indians a whit—they just moved the plays into their own backyards.

The basic roles in a pastorela are those of the shepherds, varying in number but always including the lead characters of Bato and Bartolo, and sometimes Florindo and Blas. The other indispensables are the Devil, a Hermit, and a couple of angels. Depending on the particular version, there can be many more actors . . . Lucifer sometimes has

a buffoonish assistant named Asmodeo who helps him with his evil machinations, and a horde of lesser followers besides. There may also be an Indian, a Farmer, lots more angels, and a group of shepherdesses, including Gila, Bato's wife, and one called Blanche Flor.

Bato and Bartolo represent such less-than-praiseworthy human characteristics as stupidity, extreme laziness, and gluttony. The name "Bato" once was a slang expression for "thick, lazy hick" —but actually both he and Bartolo are boors.

Bartolo is stubborn and indolent; food and sleep are his only real interests in life, and he has a tendency to doze off at important moments in the play, like the presentation of gifts to the Baby Jesus. When he is told about Christ's birth in Bethlehem, he says he sees no reason to go—he's not the godfather. He is told that he ought to go and see the ox worshiping the Christ Child; he replies that the ox might be fierce and jab him with its horn. He is told he should go because the Glory of God is there—to which he answers that if Glory wants to see him, it should come where he is. A great deal of convincing is needed to move Bartolo at all.

The Hermit, who is at least 200 years old, portrays vigorous—and feisty—old age. He does take-offs on members of the audience, while lashing out with a whip at anyone he feels is too close to him. The Farmer, or *Ranchero*, is an ordinary type, totally disinterested in religion. A simple soul, he does disrespectful things like asking Joseph to repair his pots and pans for him. The Indian is usually an object of derision—he is poor, uneducated, childlike, and speaks with a strong rural accent.

The roles are fairly interchangeable, in that the rotten characteristics of one may be given to another, if desired. Joseph, Mary, and of course the Infant Jesus, are more or less silent parts. Women sometimes play male roles, such as those of Lucifer or Michael the Archangel.

Costumes for the pastorelas are very important. There is a lot of tradition involved, but the actors are prone to add innovations as the spirit moves them. Homemade designs are the best, and can be incredibly bizarre at times. Lucifer's mask may be a violent shade of vermilion, painted on tin, or he and his fiendish cohorts

Lucifer and his demonic helper try their best to harass a shepherdess in a children's pastorela. The Angel Gabriel blows his horn and Michael the Archangel prepares to do battle with a wooden sword.

may incorporate boars' tusks or deer antlers into their headgear. Red is the only correct color for the Devil's suit nowadays—the actor playing Lucifer often looks like a rather corpulent little man wearing long red underwear. With horns and a tail.

The shepherds and shepherdesses are colorful, too, in brightly hued shirts or skirts, short capes, and straw hats decorated with mirrors, beads, gay ribbons, and flowers. Tiny bells are often sewn onto the shepherds' outfits—reminiscent of the jesters' bells of old. The Hermit is clothed in a long, hooded monk's robe, and wears a rosary—sometimes of wooden spools or squash stems. The Holy Family is allowed to wear traditional, Biblical-style clothing.

A typical pastorela might go like this. Hand-painted backdrops set the scenes. The first act may have a lurid rendering of the flames of Hell in the background. Lucifer, the Devil himself, overhears the shepherds preparing for their journey. Tail twitching with fury, he broods about what can be done to stop them. Lucifer

is obviously not at all pleased to hear that the prophecy of Christ's birth has come true. He senses trouble ahead.

That evening, as the shepherds are about to fall off to sleep, the Archangel Michael appears to warn them that the Devil is lurking nearby and, as always, is up to no good. Lucifer decides to show himself, but in disguise. He begs for food, and in passing, gets into a nasty argument with the Hermit who happens to be with the shepherds. The Devil insists that the shepherds not go, and the Hermit flies to their defense. The Archangel returns in the nick of time and leaps into a brisk sword duel with the Devil, who is finally driven away—a firecracker tied to his tail. At last the shepherds can start their journey in peace. But not for long.

From time to time the Devil reappears, trying to find out what the travelers are up to, or endeavoring to get them in trouble—tempting them through gluttony, inciting them to steal, roughing them up a bit—anything he can think of. He even lures the hapless shepherds into amorous in-

trigues with Blanche Flor, and tricks Bato and his wife Gila into matrimonial squabbles.

The Angel Gabriel appears to announce that the miraculous birth of Christ has occurred. In many productions Gabriel is lowered in a sort of lift from which he hangs suspended as he speaks to the shepherds. He then disappears—creaking—whence he came. As the play progresses, there are more arguments from Lucifer, and more defensive back talk from Michael. Gabriel, too, returns to join in the fray. Another fight ensues, this time between all the angels and the devils.

The final act sees our beleaguered shepherds at the manger in Bethlehem at last. They present the Infant Jesus with gifts —in one version they offer an extremely talkative parrot, small shirts and diapers, and a dog to watch over the Babe. The Virgin blesses them . . . upon which everyone joins in a dance, singing, and the curtain falls—but not without one last, resigned word from Lucifer: "You won, Gabriel, you won."

Mexican marketplaces at Christmastime offer a dazzling assortment of brightly colored piñatas. In a Guadalajara market, streamered comet tails in rainbow colors hang from the points of piñata stars (*right*), and bizarre animal piñatas stare over the heads of the passersby (*far right*).

Piñatas

Without doubt, one of the gayest Mexican Christmas traditions is that of the piñata, the whimsically decorated, brightly colored, hollow figure that holds candy and other goodies, and is designed expressly to be smashed to bits.

The true piñata is, underneath, a large clay pot. From that simple base, it becomes just about anything imaginable. Crepe or tissue paper, papier-mâché, tinsel, and sometimes colored paints and sequins are added, turning it into an object of sheer magic. Many piñatas nowadays are made of papier-mâché alone; the manufacturers, trying to keep up with an ever-increasing demand, found it was faster and simpler to leave out the pot.

No matter what they are made of, piñatas appear in the shape of owls, parrots, burros, peacocks, lambs, clowns, flowers, and stars —with gaily colored streamers exploding like comet trails from their points. There are Mickey Mouse and Batman piñatas, fruits and vegetables of all kinds, moons and boats and airplanes, and even piñatas in the shape of electric blenders—in purple, green, silver, gold, red, pink— every possible and often improbable combination of color and shape.

Mexico at Christmastime is a dazzling spectacle, made up in great part by the incredible array of piñatas. They are literally everywhere—in multihued ranks in the market places, hanging from lampposts and over streets, suspended overhead in every building, including churches, schools, hotels, and even airports. Piñata parties and piñata contests are held throughout the country —indoors and outdoors, in homes and in public squares, on sunny beaches, in restaurants and nightclubs. Many families enjoy making their own piñatas, buying the clay pot at the market and then having a piñata-decorating party. But whether the piñata is purchased ready-made or constructed at home, it is still an empty shell until party time approaches.

Then it is stuffed with as much candy, peanuts, fruit, and sometimes small toys as it will hold, and strung up by a rope running through a hook or pulley. One end of the rope is left free so the

Here are more examples of the various shapes piñatas might take: a fierce-looking—though homemade—devil (*top*); the Tin man (*middle*), straight out of *The Wizard of Oz*, and the truly Mexican and endearing donkey (*bottom*).

piñata can be moved up and down at will.

At a children's party, all the youngsters crowd underneath the piñata and sing a traditional verse demanding the goodies hidden inside. The hostess blindfolds one of the children and hands him a large stick, then twirls the would-be piñata breaker around —and around—until he is quite dizzy. The child tries as hard as possible to whack the piñata— but it's not where it was a second before. The adult in charge of the rope is busily raising and lowering the pot—always keeping it out of reach of the flailing stick. Three chances are allowed per person, and the onlookers shout out directions—mostly unhelpful —to the thrasher, trying to describe the location of the elusive figure.

Another child is blindfolded and given the stick for a try, then another—until finally stick and piñata connect with enough force to break the pot—and with a cracking, ripping sound a

shower of sweets comes raining down—mixed with shreds of paper and bits of clay. The youngsters scramble, shouting and grabbing for the candies, until everything has been snatched up. If by some horrid chance a child misses out on getting a treat, he or she can chant another poem asking the hostess to bring out a basket filled with more favors.

Piñata parties for adults are just as much fun, and only the singing is left out. Truly splendid grown-up-style piñatas have been created . . . and one well-to-do host outdid himself, cleverly tricking his guests in the process. As is often the case, two piñatas were provided.

Dressed to the teeth, the glittering ensemble gathered under the first piñata, chattering about one thing or another, but definitely bored by the whole childish game, and having no intention of disarranging their exquisite attire, coiffures, and self-esteem by scrambling foolishly around the floor. When the piñata broke open, tiny slips of paper with numbers written on them came fluttering down, and the host announced that if the guests would

A cluster of relatively simple but still brightly hued and shiny piñatas beckons to customers at a market in Guadalajara.

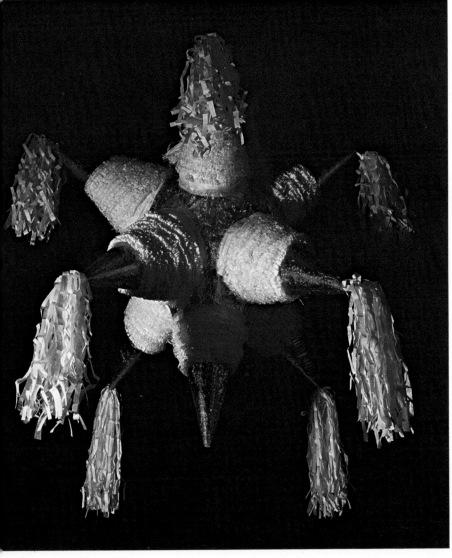

An ornate red-and-white piñata gets the star billing it richly deserves.

A papier-mâché swan piñata is under construction in this Mexico City scene. Shreds of paper mixed with glue or paste are molded into the desired shape while wet, then painted.

look in the next room they would find a surprise. The room held an incredible assortment of gifts, beautifully displayed—gold earrings, gold cuff links and rings, bracelets, costly trinkets of all kinds—which corresponded to the numbers on the slips.

As might be imagined, the breaking of the second piñata was accorded heartfelt attention. Faces upturned, bodies at the ready, the eager guests held their breath as the stick finally cracked the shell of the piñata—and out came tumbling down—a piñata-full of flour.

The piñata, like the nacimientos, came originally from Italy, where it was called *pignatta*, meaning "a fragile pot." At masquerade balls during the Renaissance period, pineapple-shaped pignattas filled with sweets were hung from ceilings and broken. The game found its way to Spain,

and was adopted there for Lent. The first Sunday of that season was called Piñata Sunday, and the piñata played a major role at Lenten masquerades and dances.

The Spanish word *piñata* referred to the game, rather than the clay pot. The container itself was called an *olla* and was, like the Italian version, left undecorated. It was not particularly attractive, and before long people began to dress it up by building a paper figure of some sort around the homely pot.

Brought to Mexico by the 16th-century missionaries, the piñata was quickly accepted by the Indians, who had a very similar custom. Toward the end of each year, the Aztec priests prepared an offering for their god of war. A clay pot filled with small treasures was covered with finely woven feathers and bright

plumes and placed upon a pole in the temple. To celebrate the anniversary of the god's birth, the pot was broken with a club and the gifts tumbled down at the feet of the idol.

Nowadays piñatas are just for fun, but long ago they were used as a religious symbol and had a serious, moral meaning. The piñata itself was supposed to represent Satan, dressed in brilliant colors to attract the innocent beholder. The treasures hidden inside were the temptations calculated to lure mankind into evil ways. The blindfolded person who tried to break the piñata represented blind faith, whose mission was to destroy evil. The stick was virtue personified . . . the goodies finally released were the reward . . . and the lesson was that all things come through faith.

In sunny Mexico, piñata parties are held everywhere during the Christmas season. This huge green-and-red parrot piñata waits for its big moment on a beach in Puerto Vallarta, Jalisco.

The children's Christmas

To children in many parts of the world, December 25 means gifts. The children of Mexico have a different tradition; their big day doesn't come until January 6. Before that, though, they don't lack for fun. Let's follow a couple of youngsters through a typical Christmas season.

Christmas for Elena and Carlos started around the first week of December when their mother unearthed the boxes of nacimiento figures. As they helped dust them off, the children decided they needed a few new additions for their Nativity scene. So early next morning they set off with María, the maid, for the market place.

Mexican markets at Christmastime are masses of bold colors and buzzing activity—noisy, jampacked, and very, very tempting. The stalls overflow with toys, candies, fruits, nacimiento figures, flowers, and piñatas. Long before dawn, tiny burros and their masters make their way along dusty roads from outlying rural districts, bearing heavy loads of wares to sell. Arriving at the market, the vendors arrange their goods in ramshackle stalls or on blankets or pieces of burlap stretched upon the ground. Greeting friends and settling down for the day, the vendors look forward with great anticipation to testing their bargaining skills on prospective buyers.

The sun was just beginning to get hot when Carlos and Elena arrived. There was a feeling of excitement in the air, and mouthwatering odors of good things to eat. They looked longingly at the pyramids of fruit—lemons, limes, mangoes, guavas, *tejocotes*—all aglow with juicy promise. Nuts and sweets of every variety beckoned: peanuts in the shell, candies wrapped in bright paper, chunks of sugar cane, candied fruit, marzipan in many shapes, and ornate scenes made entirely of sugar. Other booths offered cheeses, Christmas cakes and cookies, and sweet loaves of holiday bread.

"First things first," María said, firmly leading them off toward the stalls displaying tiny Nativity figures. Choosing what they wanted amid such a wealth of possibilities took a long time, but finally three miniature sheep were purchased, and some new shepherds to watch over them. The children and the nacimiento seller were pleased with the results of their friendly haggling.

Ringing out over the bustling hubbub came the penetrating cry of the *buñuelo* vendor, and Maria —who was getting hungry, too— gave in to the pleas of the chil-

About a week before Christmas, Nativity scenes are set up in homes throughout Mexico. Additional pieces are available in the marketplaces, as in this Oaxaca Christmas market display of saints and nacimiento figures.

Elephants, reindeer, and toothy sharks are but a few of the fanciful forms taken on by holiday piñatas. Below their frilly ranks are tempting mountains of fruits and nuts, a small part of the profusion of things to see and buy in the marketplace.

Choosing just the right piñata is a difficult decision to make. A long-necked, polka-dotted giraffe takes the fancy of a little girl at a Guadalajara market.

dren and bought three. They watched eagerly as the buñuelo woman quickly fried flat rounds of dough in hot, sizzling fat. The puffed-up, golden-brown morsels were drained, dipped in syrup, and sprinkled with pink sugar. Elena and Carlos swallowed the crisp pancakes and licked their sticky fingers. Nearby, a mariachi band was entertaining the passersby with the sound of guitars, cornets, and violins. The leader, noticing María's flashing dark brown eyes, winked at her and bowed. Elena giggled, but Carlos looked disgusted. María smiled.

Piñatas were next on the shopping list—for the youngsters' posada party on December 18th. Elena pointed out that one wouldn't be enough—two were needed, definitely. What if some-

one came late and the first one had already been broken? Making a choice was far from easy—it was even more difficult than deciding on new nacimiento figures. María sighed—it was going to be a long day. Hosts of ruffly piñatas sat side by side on shelves or hung from the tops of stalls—creatures of fantasy, unreal fruits and comic figures, absurd animals—each one had its own unique charm.

After a great deal of discussion and a near argument, the children settled on their first piñata—a lovely shocking-pink and green watermelon—which was added to María's growing burden. Carrying an unwrapped piñata home is not a simple matter. The bulky, streamered thing does not lend itself to easy transportation. All three burst into laughter as a grown man walked by just then, looking very foolish struggling with an enormous, multicolored

donkey that stuck out from under his arm.

Next, they came to a stall that sold the clay pots from which piñatas are made. Carlos announced that he wanted one—it would be even more fun to make the second piñata himself (with Elena's help). He would design a ship, or maybe a butterfly, and so they had to buy crepe paper and glue and lots of shiny sequins, too. And sweets to fill the piñatas. Carlos carried the pot; Elena volunteered to take the candy.

Shopping done—María put her foot down—the three strolled aimlessly through the market, admiring the glittering Christmas ornaments, lanterns, colored candles, straw baskets, pottery, and cheerful arrays of flowers—poinsettias, gladiolas, roses, mums, dahlias, tiger lillies, and many more. Gaudily feathered parrots

Christmas trees come in amazing varieties in Mexico. A spiky yucca cactus in Oaxaca is turned into a festive "tree" with the addition of sparkling Christmas ornaments and lights.

screeched beside songbirds in handmade rush cages, and, of course, there were toys—ceramic pigs and bulls and fat armadillos, whistles, soldiers on horseback, dolls—the children called a number of these to María's attention, hoping she might casually mention them to their parents. María didn't seem to be listening, however; it was time to go home.

On their way, they passed several houses with signs in the windows saying, "We dress the Christ Child." That sounded funny, but it just meant that a seamstress inside specialized in making lovely clothes for the nacimiento figures of the Baby Jesus.

On December 16th, the whole family helped set up the nacimiento—the newly purchased figures rounded it out nicely. The house was decorated from top to bottom, and the patio, too, with paper lanterns, fir branches, flowers, Spanish moss, and lacy paper cutouts. The neighborhood posadas began that evening, and their own, two nights later, was a huge success. Elena and Carlos loved posadas—so many parties all in a row, so many piñatas to break, so many delicious things to eat.

The last of the posadas was on Christmas Eve, *la Noche Buena.* María and their mother had both

A holiday posada ceremony (*right*) in a church in Oaxaca. Afterwards, the giant piñata is taken outside to be broken by the village children.

Children dressed as Mary and Joseph (*below*) walk in a home posada procession in Mexico City. Joseph carries a flaming sparkler on a pole.

been cooking and baking for days, and the house was full of tempting smells and activity. Because they would be staying up so late, Elena and Carlos were told to take a nap, but they were too excited to sleep, and María threw up her hands in defeat. "You'll fall asleep in church," she warned. Mid-evening, an early supper was served with more buñuelos and a holiday drink called *atole,* made of corn meal and spiced with cinnamon. Then carols were sung around the nacimiento. They had a Christmas tree, too, and Elena sniffed its pine scent with pleasure as they trouped out to join the posada.

The procession ended up at the home of their next-door neighbors . . . so afterwards both the family and their friends walked together to the cathedral for midnight Mass—the *Misa de Gallo,* or Mass of the Cock. Tall, fat candles burned in clumps of flickering light in the church, illuminating the displays of flowers; twisted crepe paper ropes hung here and there. Several nacimientos had been set up in different areas—one of wood, one of straw, and a third had amusing cartoon characters. The cathedral was overflowing—loudspeakers

broadcast the Mass to the people outside who hadn't been able to get in, and all the streets around were closed to traffic. The children and their family and friends managed to find seats . . . a good thing, too, because Carlos' head began to nod. Elena nudged him sharply with her elbow—she didn't want anyone to see him falling asleep. That would mean more naps.

The people of Mexico set off firecrackers on every holiday occasion, and Christmas Eve was no exception—the night was alive with crackling, popping noise— and Carlos was suddenly once more wide awake. As soon as they reached home, Elena reminded her brother that they must put the Infant Jesus to bed. The crib in the nacimiento had been empty since the scene was erected nine days before—waiting for the Christ Child to be born. The children sang a lullaby as Elena placed the porcelain figure in the manger atop a bed of little candies . . . and the nacimiento was complete.

Two of the shepherds, they noted, were standing very close to the center of the manger. In their house, it was customary for their parents to choose a nacimiento shepherd to represent each child. At the end of each day,

Elena's and Carlos' shepherds would be moved a step closer to the crib—if they had been good. It was a fairly effective way to induce good behavior. Elena's shepherd, however, seemed to be a step or two behind Carlos'. She decided to ignore it—Christmas was here already, and it was too late to make amends now.

The real meal of the evening came next, a sumptuous late-night Christmas feast of turkey and tortillas, fried peppers and

Concentration and determination are written all over this small girl's face (*below*) as she whacks away at a swinging, big-eared mouse piñata in Cuernavaca, Morelos.

other vegetables, fruits, candies, hot chocolate with vanilla and cinnamon, and the traditional Christmas salad of fruits, nuts, beets, and sugar cane, sprinkled with tiny colored candies.

Both Elena and Carlos slept late Christmas Day—they had, after all, stayed up until almost three in the morning. To their joy, they discovered that some small gifts had been left beside the manger scene. These were a special bonus, as the real day

for presents wouldn't be until January 6. Carlos found the whistle he had been eying in the market, and there was a familiar blue-and-white piggy bank for Elena. María did listen after all. Lots of guests came to call during the day—cousins and uncles and aunts and friends. Many brought beautiful Christmas cards that they had made themselves, and cries of *Feliz Navidad* greeted each newcomer. The garbageman

came, too, to collect his *aguinaldo*, or Christmas gift. He brought a little card wishing the family a happy and prosperous New Year and was given some money, and sweets for his children.

In the evening, the children persuaded their parents to take them for a drive to see the lights and decorations. All of Mexico blazes with lights at Christmas, and nowhere more brilliantly than in Mexico City. Millions of tiny electric bulbs twinkle and flash—on the trees in Alameda Park, all around the main square, the *Zócalo*, and in garlands suspended over the streets. Ornate designs of lights decorate the facades of buildings—some stretch 20 stories high—and vines of miniature lights cling to the prickly leaves of cactus plants. Even the traffic circles, *glorietas*, are embellished with beautiful

scenes made of lights attached to screens of netting.

Tall images of the Three Kings, the Holy Family, and Santa Claus—even an occasional reindeer or two—loom throughout the city at street corners, traffic circles, and in the stores. The Three Kings are always dressed in opulent splendor; two wear gilt crowns and the third, who is black, wears a jeweled turban. The children wanted to have their pictures taken standing next to one of these huge figures, but there were so many other cars full of people looking at the decorations that terrific traffic jams were resulting and their father couldn't possibly stop the car in the middle of all that.

Department store windows have marvelous displays, too—Carlos spotted an especially fanciful one, a winter snowscape all silver and white—but the icicles, instead of hanging down in a fringe, were poking their icy spines upwards from the ground like stalagmites.

December 28th is *El Día de los Inocentes*, the Day of the Innocents. It's sort of an April Fool's Day, and Carlos, in particular, looked forward to playing tricks on his friends. The idea is to try and fool people by borrowing money or some small treasured object from them. The borrowed

item is later replaced along with a little toy, or more often, something absolutely worthless. It took some ingenuity on Carlos' part to persuade any of his knowing friends to part with anything, but he managed.

On New Year's Eve, the children were allowed to stay up and join in the festivities. With their parents, they walked over to the main plaza to see the balloons. Thousands upon thousands of balloons were massed together in clusters of gorgeous colors and designs, some twisted into funny shapes, others painted with bizarre faces. Cars drove around and around the square, balloons bobbing from their windows. On the stroke of midnight, church bells began to ring out, drivers honked their horns, firecrackers went off, and Roman candles burst into the air. Carlos blasted away on his new whistle, adding more noise to the joyous racket. Elena held her hands over her ears, but it didn't do much good.

A crowd gathered at one side of the plaza attracted Carlos' attention. "It's El Torito," he shouted, "the little bull!" An apparently nerveless youngster, wearing an enormous headdress made of firecrackers and shaped like a bull's head, was dashing around among the spectators,

Brilliantly colored holiday balloons (*above*) being sold at Christmastime near Mexico City's Alameda. A huge street figure of one of the Three Kings (*below*) in Mexico City. Children with sparklers (*right*) during a Christmas celebration in the village church in Xoxo, Mexico.

the explosives tossing fiery sparks in every direction. The children thought it was great fun . . . but the grown-ups watched with somewhat strained smiles, trusting to the saints, no doubt, that no one would get hurt. Other children were throwing small firecrackers called "seek your feet"—they writhed about on the ground like tiny snakes. Carlos had several in his pocket and used them to make Elena jump, until a restraining hand on his shoulder—his father's—made him stop.

January 1st is a national holiday and another occasion for celebrations and feasting. Carlos and Elena stayed at home—their mother decided that they were tired, and enough was enough—besides, *El Día de los Reyes* wasn't far away.

The Day of the Three Kings, or Epiphany, falls on January 6th. In the old Bible story, three wise men, the Three Kings, brought gifts of gold, frankincense, and myrrh to the newborn Christ Child. In Mexico, the Three Kings —Caspar, Melchior, and Balthazar—bring gifts to children just like Santa Claus does in other lands.

On the evening of January 5th, Elena and Carlos hovered anxiously around their parents until they were given permission to set out a pair of empty shoes on the balcony. Elena took some of the straw from the nacimiento and tucked it into each shoe—an offering for the camels the Three Kings come ariding on. It was very difficult to get to sleep that night. Weeks earlier they had written letters to the Three Kings, telling them what they wanted most, and impressing upon them that they had been good. Bad children, traditionally, are likely to find chunks of coal in their shoes—an unpleasant prospect.

Next morning, the straw was gone! The children could no longer even see the shoes—they were buried under a marvelous pile of presents. Games, wind-up toys, candy, fruits, and peanuts—everything they had asked for was there—and not one bit of coal. They hoped the camels had enjoyed the straw.

Late that afternoon, the youngsters raced off ahead of their parents to their friend Juan's house. Juan's father and mother had been chosen to be the godparents for the Christ Child at the Christmas Eve posada, which meant they had to give a party on this day. Everyone described the presents they had received, and there was even another piñata. Along with the good things to eat

was a special ring-shaped cake called *La Rosca de Reyes*, the Kings' Ring. Juan's mother sliced the cake and warned the young people to be careful when they bit into it. A small doll representing the Christ Child is baked into the cake—whoever finds it may keep it, and is then expected to give a party for his or her friends on February 2nd, *El Día de la Candelaria*.

Elena tasted her slice cautiously, took a second bite, and shouted gleefully, "I found it! You're all invited to my house next month!"

It might seem a long time after Christmas, but *El Día de la Candelaria*, or Candlemas, is still part of the holiday season, and eventually February 2nd arrived. Candlemas is a noisy holiday, the occasion—as usual—for still more fireworks, including impressive, large set pieces that when ignited portray all manner of scenes—historic, dramatic, or just for fun.

The most ingenious of these is the *castillo*, or castle. Painstakingly put together on a metal, towerlike frame, the castillo may have images of Spanish soldiers spinning around the battlements, cannons firing, rows of pinwheels set off one at a time sending waterfalls of color cascading down, all ending in a grand finale

of rockets whooshing into the air, bursting into myriads of multi-colored sparks and echoing explosions of sound.

Late Candlemas afternoon, Elena's guests and many of their parents gathered for her party; and after all the games had been played and all the refreshments gobbled up, the ceremony of the manger began. The children formed a procession and marched into the room where the Christ Child lay sleeping in His crib.

One of the girls, called a *comadre*, approached the manger and gently picked up the little image of the Infant Jesus. Dressing it in silken robes, she placed a tiny halo over its head and laid it on a tray adorned with flowers and candles that had been specially blessed for that day. The admiring guests gathered around and kissed the Babe, and another procession formed—this time leading out of the house toward the church. There the priest blessed the image of the Christ Child . . . and the group escorted it back to Elena's where, with the rest of the nacimiento figures, it was packed away for another year.

Candlemas—and the holidays—had come to an end.

On the Feast of Three Kings, January 6, a special cake called *La Rosca de Reyes*, The Kings' Ring, is served. At this party (*below*), each child is hoping to find the little image of the Christ Child baked inside. A child (*bottom left*) asks one of the Three Kings for a present. Photographers hire men costumed as the Three Kings to pose with customers. Holiday fireworks explode from a "castillo" (castle) framework in Cuernavaca (*right*).

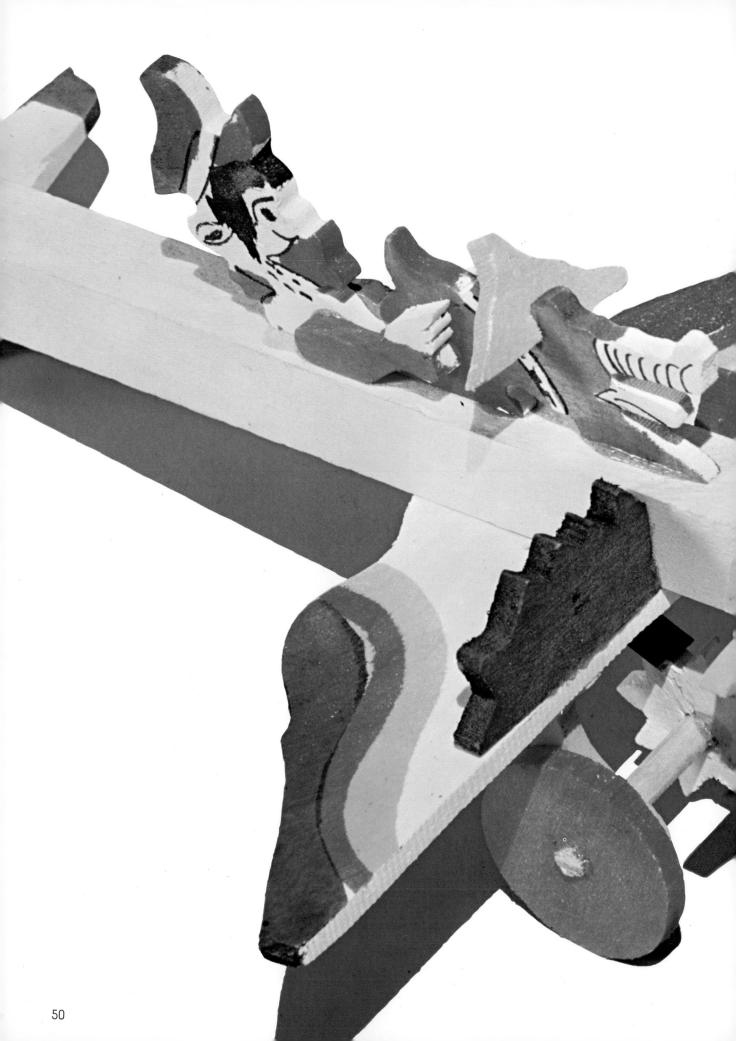

In Mexico, toys and other presents are usually given to the children of the house on January 6, the Feast of the Three Kings. As elsewhere, many Mexican toys today are mass produced, but certain regions still specialize in delightful handcrafted items.

A painted wooden airplane from Irapuato, Guanajuato.

Painted papier-mâché figures of men on horseback from Celaya, Guanajuato.

The figure of a man riding a bull (*left*), from Puebla, is woven from a particular type of straw made from palm leaves. Brightly painted wooden guitars, violins, and boxes (*right top*) are from Paracho, Michoacán; and from Salatitán, Jalisco, come amusing and colorful clay whistles (*below right*).

During the holiday season, all Mexico celebrates with traditional dances and observances, each region in its own way. At this village party in San Juan Teotihuacán, townsfolk dress up in ornate costumes, including representations of the evil Moors.

Christmas celebrations here and there

Mexico is a land of striking diversity; its topography ranges from soaring, snow-capped mountains to tropical jungles, from high plateaus to sun-drenched beaches. Ancient Aztec and Mayan ruins vie for attention with ultramodern architecture, sleepy villages with sophisticated cities. The country's holiday observances vary from the devoutly solemn to gorgeous pageantry and spirited foolishness—and never are the celebrations so colorful as during the Christmas season. Special holiday events are held throughout Mexico, so come along on a tour of some of the regional happenings in this land of fiestas. . . .

Traveling to the east coast of Mexico, we might join the people of Santiago Tuxla, Veracruz, in celebrating the season with Christmas songs called *Pascuas*, and visits to manger scenes in every neighborhood. Here also the quaint custom of *La Rama*, the branch, is practiced. A real branch is decorated with paper chains and strips of colored paper, ribbons, Japanese lanterns, and small clay figures of shepherds, donkeys, angels, and the like. Accompanied by musicians—sometimes playing instruments made from tin cans— the branch is carried from door to door, the bearers singing traditional verses demanding *aguinaldos* (gifts) of money, fruits, or candies.

When a homeowner is a bit slow in coming up with the aguinaldo, he is serenaded thusly: "Give me my Christmas gift if you mean to give; the night is long and we have far to walk." Those quick to donate are graciously thanked: "I sing for you at Christmas, not for your money but in the name of the saints in Heaven, and with as much joy as that of the Virgin Mary. The branch is leaving now—very grateful—because it was well received in this house." Stingy types who give nothing are shamed by jeers and a final insult—"The branch is leaving now, very upset, because it has not received anything in this place. The branch is leaving now without anything on, because in this house they are miserably poor."

Veracruz also offers a dance exhibition called the *huapango*. It takes place on a raised wooden platform, sometimes laid over hollow clay jars for added resonance. As the music begins, the young men step in front of the girls with whom they wish to dance, and silently raise their hats. The girls follow them onto the dance floor, and two lines are formed. Bodies are kept rigid as the dancers pass one another, and then exchange places. A stamp of the heel is followed by two taps with the toe, accented by the musicians slapping the strings of their instruments with their open hands. *El Caimán* and *La Bamba* are both specialities of this region, too—dancers balance a glass of water or bottle of liquor on their heads, and somehow manage to tie a knot in a sash with their feet—while still dancing.

In Querétaro, in the plateau region northwest of Mexico City, Christmas parades are an annual occurrence. Seventy-four arches spanning the picturesque city form a graceful setting for the processions and countless stalls bursting with things to buy line

A masked dancer in a huge
feathered headdress takes part
in a performance by the
Tacotines Indians of Puebla.

the way. From December 6th to
the 22nd, nightly parades pass
through the streets with bands,
lanterns, torches; feather-plumed
dancers leaping and posturing;
charros and *chinas* (village
dandies and beauties) astride
richly ornamented horses;
medieval heralds; and small
boys representing dwarfs wearing huge, grotesquely painted
heads.

On December 23rd, a series of
Biblical floats built on platforms
atop cars ends up that evening's
parade. All through the year, a
committee has been working on
plans for the floats, and they are
always memorable. Involved

pageants are acted out on each
one, portraying scenes of Para-
dise, Jacob's Ladder, the Feast of
Balthazar, Solomon's Judgment,
and more. Brilliantly arrayed
actors emote, sing, and dance;
real animals enact their roles
with enthusiasm—donkeys bray,
ducks quack, dogs bark, parrots
squawk. And over all comes the
sound of church bells ringing,
and crackling, banging salvos of
fireworks.

Michoacán, west of Mexico
City, has a town called Tzintzuntzan, meaning Place of the
Hummingbird. One of its most
popular dances is *Las Sembradoras* (The Sowers), performed for Candlemas. It's a
dance of thanksgiving for the
bountiful harvest just gathered
and a prayer for the crop to come.
The male dancers carry hoes and
shovels, the women, baskets of
wheat or corn from which they
toss samples to the audience.

White shirts and embroidered
pants with stunning black-and-

white fringed serapes over their
shoulders are worn by the men.
The women, their braids entwined
with ribbons, perform in embroidered blouses and wide,
sashed skirts that are straight in
front and pleated behind, and
blue-and-white striped rebozos.
The couples dance around a yoke
of oxen decorated with ears of
corn, ribbons, and flowers, and
the women scatter flower petals
over the ground as though they
were sowing in the fields.

The humorous *Viejitos* is
danced throughout Michoacán
—young men make themselves
up to look as old as possible and
enact the roles of little old men.
Dressed in white suits with embroidered cuffs, they wear flat,
wide-brimmed hats and wooden
masks that grin toothlessly. Each
carries a staff and tries to out-
clown the others in pretending to
be decrepit and ancient, leaping
with great agility into the air

Dances by Santiagos Matamoros,
like the one in this picture, are
part of Christmas festivities in
San Juan Amuzgo, Oaxaca.

Moors and Christians battle it out
in the popular *matachín* dance-
drama, performed here by the
Tarahumara Indians in Nara-
rachi, Chihuahua.

One of the lavishly decorated floats (*right*) that take part in the calenda processions held in Oaxaca on December 24. On the previous evening, known as The Night of the Radishes, a contest for the best radish carving (*below right*) is held in the city's main square.

from time to time, then reverting to the stiff-jointed movements of advanced old age.

Los Moros y Cristianos, the *Santiagos*, and the *matachines* dances may be seen in many regions of Mexico. Classical dance-dramas with elaborate costumes, they relate the battles between the Moors and Christians, with much clashing of wooden swords—and the Moors always lose.

Crockery smashing and weirdly carved radishes may sound like an unlikely combination, but they are Christmas-week traditions in Oaxaca, 340 miles southeast of Mexico City. A three-day festival honoring the Virgin of Solitude, patron saint of the city and state of Oaxaca, starts things off on December 19th. Buñuelo vendors sell their wares on crockery saucers, which, according to custom, are hurled into the air to smash into bits on the ground below—for good luck in the coming year. By the end of the evening, the shards are almost ankle-deep.

December 23rd is *la Noche de los Rábanos*, the Night of the

The ritual of "Pedido de la Cruz" or "Cross of Petition" (*far left*). In a small village near Mitla, Oaxaca, the people gather at midnight on New Year's Eve and "spell" their wishes for the coming year. Close-up of masked Santiago dancer (*left*) in the village of Atempan, Puebla.

Radishes. All around the plaza, gaily decorated stalls display enormous radishes. Carved into an amazing array of shapes, the radishes are turned into religious scenes, landscapes, replicas of bullfights, skillful reproductions of devils, men riding horses, elephants, or burros— even a radish Apollo XI display complete with astronauts and spaceships appeared one year. No one eats the radishes—they're much too strong. Instead, the imaginative figures are carefully judged, and, after prizes have been awarded, are sold.

Processions called *calendas* form after the last posada in Oaxaca, on December 24th. Each of the city's 35 churches invites a lady, preferably well-to-do, to be the godmother of the Infant Jesus. She donates money for lanterns and fireworks. On Christmas Eve, the godmother carries an image of the Child on a cushioned tray to the main square, all the neighbors following behind. There the different calendas meet and then proceed to their own churches where the priest receives them. The godmother places the Child upon the manger, and the Mass begins. The many calenda processions crisscrossing the city at night make an unforgettable sight with their bobbing lantern lights . . . houses along the routes are adorned with strips of colored paper and flowers, and women in the processions carry baskets on their heads holding intricate figures of swans, miniature gardens, ships, and lyres, all made of flowers.

The *Pedido de la Cruz*, or Cross of Petition, is the New Year's Eve custom in Mitla, Oaxaca. The Zapotec Indians gather at a stone cross to pray and make offerings of flowers and candles, and blow incense to the four winds. Then they place upon the ground houses or animals made of sticks, farm implements made of twigs or seeds, or little piles of stones signifying a husband, wife, or children—whatever it is they want the most. The Indians believe that a wish made on that night will be granted—if it is not, they must not have deserved it— but there's always the next year.

Mayan and Christian beliefs come together in a five-day year-end carnival in Chamula, in Mexico's southern highlands. Villagers called Passions represent both Christ and the sun god. Others act out the roles of evil monkeys dressed in tall, beribboned fur hats—they symbolize Christ's persecutors and the enemies of the sun. On the fourth day, both Passions and Monkeys dance over a flaming patch of ground, showing repentance— and pleasing the gods besides.

Throughout the land, the customs of the past and those of the present continue to flourish, amicably joined in the Christmastime celebrations of this unique country.

Mexico's Christmas gifts to the world

Many of Mexico's Christmas traditions, like the piñatas and posadas, came from Old Spain. But several of its Christmas symbols were native born, and have since traveled from Mexico to other parts of the world.

First among these is the most popular Christmas flower of all, the poinsettia. An old Mexican legend tells of a little boy who wanted more than anything to visit the manger in his village church. He was very poor and had no gift to bring to the tiny Christ Child, and he felt sad. Along the way, he noticed a bush growing beside the dusty road, and thought he could at least take a few of its green branches to present to the newborn Babe.

Miraculously, as soon as he had cut them, the branches sprouted scarlet, star-shaped flowers . . . and the boy had a lovely gift for the Infant Jesus. He ran to the church and laid the flowers at the foot of the crib, upon which the Virgin Mother raised her hand in a gesture of love. The golden stars on her robe began to twinkle, and outside in the dark, velvety sky a bright star appeared in the east and shone down in splendor over the little Mexican village. The flower was called *Flor de la Noche Buena*, or Flower of Christmas Eve.

Another story about the origin of the poinsettia is a more melancholy one. A young girl, separated from her lover, died of a broken heart on Christmas Eve. The drops of blood which fell to the earth were transformed into the huge red flowers of the poinsettia.

Whatever you wish to believe, the poinsettia has been around a long time. The Aztecs knew it, but only as one of the many beautiful flowers that grew in the hot climate of Mexico. They called it *cuetlaxóchitl*, the flower of purity. During colonial times in Mexico, people noticed that the poinsettia bloomed only in December, and so associated it with the birth of Christ and used it to decorate their Christmas Nativity scenes.

In 1825, Dr. Joel Robert Poinsett, the first American ambassador to Mexico and an amateur botanist, admired the flower and called the blooms "flame leaves." He sent cuttings home to his greenhouses in South Carolina. A nurseryman in Philadelphia later named it *Euphorbia poinsettia*, or *Poinsettia pulcherrima*, after Dr. Poinsett. Albert Ecke first raised it commercially in the United States on

his farm near Los Angeles, and that region of California is now called the *Poinsettia Belt,* as it supplies much of the country with the plants.

Christmas dinner would be nothing without its main attraction, a golden roast turkey, redolent with good smells and stuffed to overflowing. We associate turkey with Thanksgiving and the Pilgrims, but it was known in Mexico long before the Mayflower landed in Massachusetts. Hernan Cortés observed the birds when he arrived in Mexico in the 16th century and was intrigued by the way they wandered around loose in Montezuma's palace. He promptly had some captured and sent home to the king in Spain. The original flock grew, and turkeys were exported to other parts of Europe.

Only nobility could feast on the rare bird, however. In Venice, the ruling Council of Ten decided which families would be allowed to eat turkey, and it was very expensive indeed. Francis I, the king of France, was the only person in that country who could have it at all. He wasn't totally selfish, however—he would occasionally toss morsels of turkey to his courtiers to taste. Turkey today is eaten regularly in many parts of the world, and in Mexico it is a traditional part of the Christmas Eve dinner.

The third gift, of course, is chocolate itself, an essential element of Mexican Christmas feasts. And again it was Cortés who first tasted it in Mexico and shared it with the world. In 1519, Emperor Montezuma served a drink called *chocolatl* to his Spanish guests—in great, golden goblets. The Spaniards didn't like it very well, actually—it was bitter, but Cortés once commented in a letter, "A cup of this drink is enough to keep a man going all day." The Indians themselves sometimes used red pepper and corn meal to give more flavor to the beverage.

Cortés and other of his countrymen discovered that the stuff tasted better when sweetened with sugar. Back in Spain, cinnamon and vanilla were added, too, and someone had the idea that it would be even more delicious if served hot. It was. Chocolate drinking spread from the Spanish aristocracy to the court of France, across the channel to Great Britain—and eventually to the cocoa mugs of the common people everywhere.

Add a Mexican touch to your Christmas

Food, fun, and song are important parts of Christmas celebrations everywhere. In Mexico, they take on added color and gaity. On the following pages, you will find a selection of recipes, projects, and songs chosen especially to bring the festive flavor of the Mexican Christmas into your home.

Mexican cuisine is as varied as any in the world, and it is not always hot! Some of the dishes can be traced back to the Mayas and the Aztecs, others are contributions of the Spaniards, the French, or the Americans. There are also many regional variants in Mexican cooking. The culinary sampler in this book includes typical Christmas dishes from different parts of the country.

The easy-to-make projects include a star piñata for a festive piñata-smashing party, an ornament called "Ojo de Dios" ("God's Eye"), and a yarn-wrapped animal toy, all designed for family participation.

For a truly Mexican Christmas, plan a posada party with the piñata as its high point. Five posada songs are presented here for singing along as the Holy Pilgrims look for lodgings, are turned away by several heartless innkeepers, and finally, to everybody's joy, are given shelter. *Feliz Navidad y Feliz Año Nuevo!*

Recipes

Pozole

2 pork hocks, split into two or three pieces each
1 large onion, sliced
2 cloves garlic, minced
Water
1 stewing chicken, cut in serving pieces
1 pound pork loin, boneless, cut in 1-inch chunks
2 cups canned hominy or canned garbanzos
1 teaspoon salt
½ teaspoon pepper
1 cup sliced crisp radishes
1 cup shredded cabbage
1 cup shredded lettuce
½ cup chopped green onions
Lime or lemon wedges

1. Put split pork hocks, onion, and garlic into a kettle, cover with water and cook until almost tender (about 3 hours).

2. Add chicken and pork loin and cook 45 minutes, or until chicken is almost tender.

3. Add hominy, salt, and pepper. Cook about 15 minutes, or until all meat is tender.

4. Remove pork hocks and chicken from soup. Remove meat from bones and return meat to soup.

5. Serve in large soup bowls. Accompany with a relish tray offering the radishes, cabbage, lettuce, green onions, and lime or lemon wedges as garnishes.

8 to 10 servings

Red Snapper Veracruz Style

¼ cup olive oil
1 cup chopped onion
1 clove garlic, minced
2 cups (16-ounce can) tomatoes with liquid
1 teaspoon salt
¼ teaspoon pepper
2 pounds red snapper filets
¼ cup sliced pimento-stuffed olives
2 tablespoons capers
Lemon wedges

1. Heat oil in a large skillet. Cook onion and garlic in hot oil until onion is soft (about 5 minutes). Add tomatoes, salt, and pepper and cook about 5 minutes to blend flavors; slightly chop tomatoes as they cook.

2. Arrange red snapper filets in a 3-quart baking dish. Pour sauce over fish. Sprinkle with olives and capers.

3. Bake at 350°F. for 25 to 30 minutes, or until fish can be flaked easily with a fork. Serve with lemon wedges.

About 6 servings

Empanadas

Filling:
½ pound beef, coarsely chopped
½ pound pork, coarsely chopped
½ cup chopped onion
1 small clove garlic, minced
½ cup chopped raw apple
¾ cup chopped tomatoes
¼ cup raisins
¾ teaspoon salt
⅛ teaspoon pepper
Dash ground cinnamon
Dash ground cloves
¼ cup almonds, chopped
Pastry:
4 cups all-purpose flour
1¼ teaspoons salt
1⅓ cups lard or shortening
⅔ cup icy cold water

1. For filling, cook beef and pork together in large skillet until well browned. Add onion and garlic and cook until onion is soft. Add remaining ingredients, except almonds, and simmer 15 to 20 minutes.

2. Stir in almonds. Cool.

3. For pastry, mix flour and

salt in a bowl. Cut in lard until mixture resembles coarse crumbs. Sprinkle water over flour mixture, stirring lightly with a fork until all dry ingredients hold together. Divide dough in 4 portions.

4. On a lightly floured surface, roll one portion of dough at a time to ⅛-inch thickness.

5. Cut 5-inch rounds of pastry with a knife. Place a rounded spoonful of filling in center of each round. Fold and seal each round by dampening inside edges of pastry and pressing together with tines of fork.

6. Place empanadas on a baking sheet. Bake at 400°F. for 15 to 20 minutes, or until lightly browned. Or fry in fat for deep frying heated to 365°F. until browned (about 3 minutes); turn once.

    24 to 30 empanadas

Sweet Tamales

3½ dozen large dry corn husks
    (or 4″ x 9″ squares of parchment paper or foil)
1 cup lard (or ½ cup lard and
    ½ cup butter or margarine)
4 cups dehydrated masa flour
    (masa harina)
1 cup sugar
1 teaspoon salt
2½ to 3 cups warm water or
    fruit juice
Date-Pecan Filling (or other fruit
    or nut filling of your choice)

1. Wash corn husks in warm water, place in pan and cover with boiling water. Let soak at least 30 minutes before using.

2. Beat lard until light and fluffy, using spoon or electric mixer.

3. Combine masa flour, sugar, and salt. Gradually beat this mixture and water into lard until dough sticks together and has a paste-like consistency.

4. Shake excess water from each softened corn husk and pat dry on paper towels. Spread about 2 tablespoons tamale dough on center portion of husk, leaving at least a 2-inch margin at both ends and about ½-inch margin at right side. Spoon about 1½ tablespoons filling onto dough. Wrap tamale, overlapping left side first, then right side slightly over left. Fold bottom up and top down.

5. Lay tamales in top section of steamer with open flaps on bottom. (If husks are too short to stay closed, they may be tied with string or thin strips of corn husk.) Tamales may completely fill top section of steamer but should be placed so there are spaces between them for circulation of steam.

6. Steam over simmering water about 1 hour, or until corn husks can be peeled from dough easily.

    3½ dozen tamales

Date-Pecan Filling: Blend 1 cup brown sugar, ¼ cup butter or margarine, and ½ teaspoon cinnamon until smooth. Add 1 cup

chopped pitted dates and 1 cup chopped pecans; toss until evenly mixed.

Torrejas de Coco
Mexican-style French toast served at *posadas.*

1 cup sugar
½ cup water
1 coconut, drained, shelled,
    pared, and shredded
1 (1½-pound) loaf egg bread,
    sliced
3 eggs
1 tablespoon flour
1 cup lard
3 cups sugar
1 cinnamon stick
1 cup water
3 tablespoons raisins
¼ cup pinenuts or chopped
    blanched almonds

1. Dissolve 1 cup of sugar in ½ cup of water in a saucepan over medium heat. Bring to boiling; boil 3 minutes. Add shredded coconut; let it cook until moisture is absorbed and coconut is dry (about 15 minutes). Remove from heat and cool slightly.

2. Put coconut paste between each two slices of egg bread.

3. Beat eggs with flour; dip both sides of sandwiches in egg and fry in lard in a skillet (about 1 minute on each side). Drain them on absorbent paper.

4. Make a syrup by heating 3 cups sugar, cinnamon, and 1 cup

water to boiling in a large skillet; boil 5 minutes. Add browned sandwiches and simmer several minutes; turn once.

5. Arrange on a serving dish, garnish with raisins and pine-nuts, and strain the syrup over all.

About 12 servings

Nut Cookies

 1 cup butter or margarine
¾ cup confectioners' sugar
 2 cups all-purpose flour, sifted
¾ cup nuts, chopped

1. Beat butter until creamy. Add sugar, mixing until light and fluffy.

2. Stir in flour and nuts; mix well.

3. Shape into 1-inch balls.

4. Bake on greased baking sheet in preheated moderate oven (350°F.) for 12 to 15 minutes.

5. Remove from oven while still warm.

6. Roll cookies in additional confectioners' sugar. Cool completely on wire rack.

About 4 dozen cookies

Chestnut Cake

 1 cup butter or margarine
1¼ cups sugar
 6 eggs, separated
1¼ cups all-purpose flour, sifted
 1 teaspoon baking powder
½ teaspoon salt
½ cup milk
½ teaspoon vanilla
1½ cups chestnuts, chopped

1. Cream butter and sugar until light and fluffy.

2. Add egg yolks one at a time, beating well after each addition.

3. Sift together flour, baking powder, and salt. Add sifted dry ingredients alternately with milk.

4. Stir in vanilla and nuts.

5. Beat egg whites until stiff. Gently fold into cake batter.

6. Pour batter into 2 well-greased and floured 9-inch cake pans.

7. Bake in preheated moderate oven (350°F.) for 30 to 35 minutes.

Apricot-filled Pastries

 1 cup dried apricots
 1 cup water
½ cup sugar
½ teaspoon vanilla extract
 2 cups all-purpose flour
¾ teaspoon salt
½ teaspoon baking powder
⅔ cup lard
 4 to 6 tablespoons icy cold water
Confectioners' Sugar Glaze

1. Put apricots and water into saucepan. Cover, bring to a boil, and cook 20 minutes.

2. Turn contents of saucepan into an electric blender; cover and blend until smooth.

3. Combine blended apricots and sugar in saucepan; cook until thick (about 5 minutes). Cool slightly; stir in vanilla extract.

4. Mix flour, salt, and baking powder in a bowl. Cut in lard until crumbly. Add cold water, 1 tablespoon at a time, tossing with a fork until dough holds

together. Divide in half.

5. Roll each half of dough to a 14 x 10-inch rectangle on a lightly floured surface.

6. Line a baking pan with one rectangle of dough. Spread apricot mixture evenly over dough. Place remaining dough on top; seal edges. Prick top crust.

7. Bake at 400°F. for 25 minutes, or until lightly browned around edges.

8. Cool slightly. Frost with Confectioners' Sugar Glaze. Cut in squares.

2 dozen filled pastries
Confectioners' Sugar Glaze: Combine 1 cup confectioners' sugar and ½ teaspoon vanilla extract. Blend in milk or cream (about 3 tablespoons) until glaze is of spreading consistency.

Buñuelos

 4 cups all-purpose flour
 2 tablespoons sugar
 1 teaspoon baking powder
 1 teaspoon salt
 2 eggs, well beaten
¾ to 1 cup milk
¼ cup butter or margarine, melted
Oil for deep frying, heated to 350°F.
Granulated sugar-cinnamon mixture for dusting

1. Mix flour with sugar, baking powder, and salt in a bowl.

2. Combine beaten eggs and ¾ cup of the milk. Stir into dry ingredients to make a stiff dough; add more milk if needed to moisten all dry ingredients. Stir in butter or margarine.

3. Turn dough onto a lightly floured surface and knead 1 to 2 minutes until smooth. Divide dough into 24 balls. Roll each ball into a round shape about 6 inches in diameter.

4. Fry each buñuelo in hot deep fat until delicately browned, turning to fry on second side. Drain on absorbent paper. Sprinkle with sugar-cinnamon mixture while still warm.

2 dozen buñuelos

Candied Pumpkin
1 pumpkin (about 6½ pounds)
4½ cups firmly packed brown sugar
1 cup water
2 oranges, juice and shredded peel
1¾ cups nuts, chopped

1. Pare, remove seedy center, and shred pumpkin.

2. Combine brown sugar and water in a large saucepan; heat until syrup starts to thicken.

3. Add pumpkin to syrup and cook slowly, stirring constantly.

4. When thickened, add orange juice and shredded orange peel; cook until thickened, then add nuts.

5. Put candied pumpkin into a serving dish. Let cool about 3 hours.

Capirotada
2 cups firmly packed dark brown sugar
1 quart water
1 stick cinnamon
1 clove
6 slices toast, cubed
3 apples, pared, cored, and sliced
1 cup raisins
1 cup blanched almonds, chopped
½ pound Monterey Jack or similar cheese, cubed

1. Put brown sugar, water, cinnamon, and clove into a saucepan and bring to a boil, reduce heat, and simmer until a light syrup is formed. Discard spices and set syrup aside.

2. Meanwhile, arrange a layer of toast cubes in a buttered casserole dish. Cover with a

layer of apples, raisins, almonds, and cheese. Repeat until all ingredients are used. Pour syrup over all.

3. Bake at 350°F. for about 30 minutes.

4. Serve hot.

6 servings

Hot Mexican Eggnog
1 quart milk
8 egg yolks
½ cup sugar
1½ teaspoons shredded orange peel
1½ cups brandy (cognac)
Ground cinnamon

1. Scald milk.

2. Mix egg yolks and sugar in a bowl. Add scalded milk gradually, stirring constantly. Pour into top of a large double boiler. Cook over boiling water, stirring constantly until mixture coats a spoon.

3. Remove from water. Add orange peel and brandy.

4. Mix, a small amount at a time, in an electric blender until foamy.

5. Serve hot in punch cups. Sprinkle with cinnamon.

About 7 cups

Ornaments

Wrapped yarn animals

Colorful little animals like this one are made in many villages in Mexico. The body of the animal is often made of pottery, but papier-mâché can also be used. You can make a wrapped yarn animal in just a few simple steps.

1. Start by crumpling up sheets of newspaper. Then cut long, thin strips of newspaper. Coat one side of the strips with Elmer's glue. Wrap the strips tightly around the crumpled newspaper until the pieces are shaped the way you want them. Let the pieces dry.

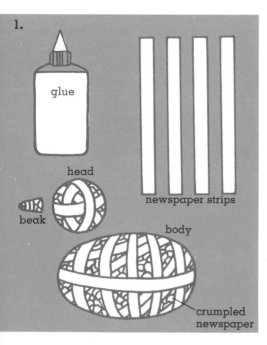

2. Glue the pieces together to make the animal shape. Let the animal dry.

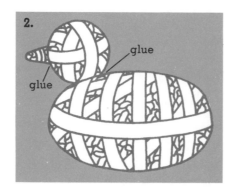

3. Cover the whole animal with glue. Cut thin strips of paper towelling and wrap them onto the body. Keep putting on layers of glue and strips of paper towelling until the animal has a smooth, white surface. Use lots of glue. Let the animal dry.

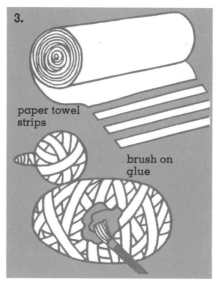

4. Glue brightly colored yarn onto the body. The yarn should lie in neat rows, each yarn right next to the one before it. Do only a small area at a time. You might want to use T-pins to help hold the yarn in place while it dries.

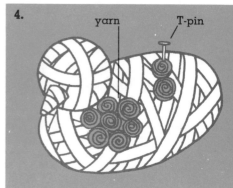

5. Make any designs you like with the yarn. Curved designs such as circles, ovals, leaves, and flowers are easiest to make.

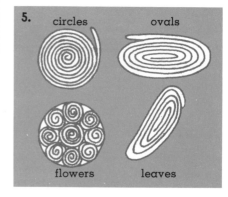

Ojo de Dios

The *ojo de Dios* (God's eye) has been made by the Indians of Mexico and Central America for hundreds of years. The diamond pattern is the symbol of the eye of God. The bands of color around the central diamond are said to symbolize the wisdom and light coming from the eye.

To make an ojo de Dios, you will need two smooth sticks (ice cream sticks or thin dowels) and at least three colors of yarn. Mexicans like to use strong, bright colors.

1. Now make a cross with the two sticks. Choose the color that will be in the middle of the eye. With one end of the yarn, tie the cross in place, using square knots.

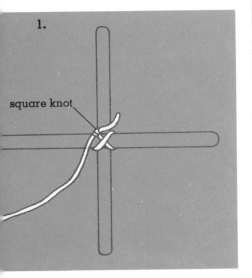

square knot

2. Start winding the yarn around the crossed sticks. Follow the winding pattern in this diagram. Hold the yarn fairly tight as you wind it.

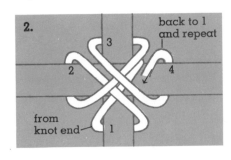

2.

3

back to 1 and repeat

2

4

from knot end

1

3. Keep winding around the sticks. Let the buildup of yarn cover up the loose ends. As you wind, lay each yarn down next to the yarn before it. The yarn should lie in neat rows.

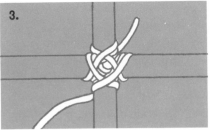

3.

4. To change colors, put the end of the first-color and the beginning of the second-color yarn behind one of the sticks. Hold the two yarns in place with your thumb. Start winding the second color. After you have wound the second color around twice, the yarn ends will be held in place.

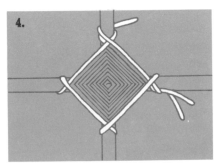

4.

5. Keep winding the yarn on and making patterns with the colors. Stop winding a little before you get to the end of the stick. If you like, you can tie pompoms on the ends of the sticks.

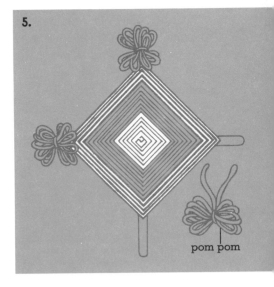

5.

pom pom

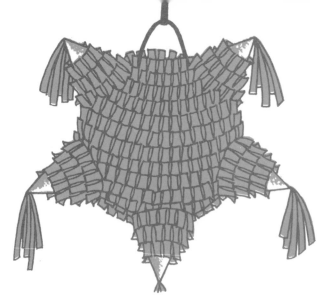

Star piñata

1 round balloon that can be in-
flated to 11″
newspaper that has been torn into
strips about 2 inches wide
liquid starch or flour-and-water
paste made from one part flour
and two parts water
10 feet of heavy cord
1 package of tissue paper, 20″ x
30″
1 sheet of aluminum foil, 12″ x 12″
masking tape
rubber cement

1. Inflate an oval or round balloon to about 11″ in diameter and
knot the end. Tear the newspaper
into strips about 2 inches wide.
Do not cut the papers; torn strips
will adhere to each other much
better. Dip the strips into liquid
starch or paste, wipe off the excess, and lay onto the balloon. Al-

ternate the direction in which you
apply the strips, as it is easier to
remember how many layers you
have put on and it will give
strength to the piñata. Lay the
balloon on a newspaper while
you apply the strips and it will be
easier to hold. Apply four layers
of newspaper strips. Leave a 2″ x
2″ uncovered area near stem end
for piñata opening. Allow to dry
about 3 days.

Deflate balloon when piñata is
thoroughly dried; the balloon will
fall away from the inside and can
be discarded.

2. To make cones for five points
of star, follow the pattern shown
in the diagram. Cut five cones out
of heavy typing paper, each
measuring 8″ on straight sides as
shown. Do not form cone shapes
yet. Following pattern for cone
tip, cut five tips of aluminum foil,
each measuring 4″ on straight
sides as shown. Spread rubber cement on one side of every tip. Cement tips onto the cut cones at the
narrow end of the cone. Form the
five cones by overlapping the
straight edges on each one, putting a staple about 2 inches from
the bottom, and cementing the
edges together.

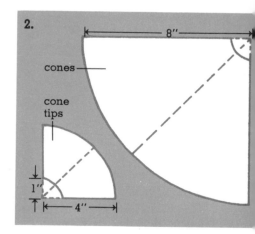

3. Make 1″ cuts around bottom
edges of every cone. Fold back
these cut edges and, beginning at
bottom edge of piñata opening,
attach the five cones in a straight
line around the piñata form, using
masking tape.

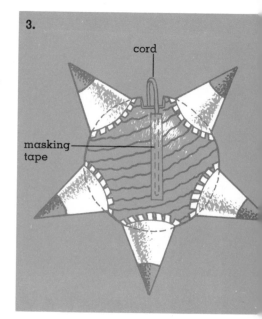

Attach cord harness securely with masking tape around the fullest part of the form. Be sure to leave ends of harness, near piñata opening, so that a suspension rope may be tied to it.

4. Prepare the tissue paper fringe. Cut the folded sheets of tissue paper crosswise into strips three inches wide. Each strip will be 3″ x 30″. Fold groups of 4 or 5 strips in half lengthwise. Fringe the strip by cutting from the open edge to within ½″ of the fold. These slashes should be approximately ⅛″ to ³⁄₁₆″ apart. Spread

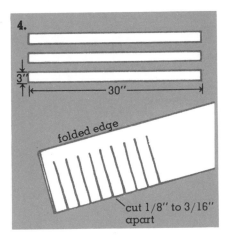

4.

3″

30″

folded edge

cut 1/8″ to 3/16″ apart

newspapers on your work area. Separate the groups of 4 or 5 strips of fringe into single strips. With a small brush, spread rubber cement along one edge of the ruffle.Unlike water-base adhesives, rubber cement will do the job without causing colors to run

and tissue paper to crinkle. Apply the fringe, beginning at the bottom of the piñata in such a way that only the actual fringe of the preceding row is visible.

5. When the fringe is being applied, stand the piñata form on an empty 3-lb. coffee can. Apply fringe until the piñata is completely covered except for the opening at the top. Secure cords at edge of opening to piñata so that they do not pull off tissue paper fringe. Apply tissue fringe also from the base of aluminum cone tips to base of cones. To make tassels, cut tissue paper into strips ¼″ x 3½″. Divide them into five equal bunches and attach one bunch to every cone tip with rubber cement.

6. To fill opening of piñata, flatten strips of cut tissue paper fringe and roll until you have a flowerlike section large enough so that it will not fall through opening. Tie the bottom of the roll with string.

Fill with candy or small toys and suspend from the ceiling.

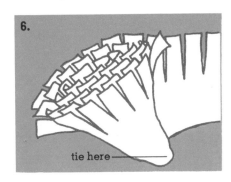

6.

tie here

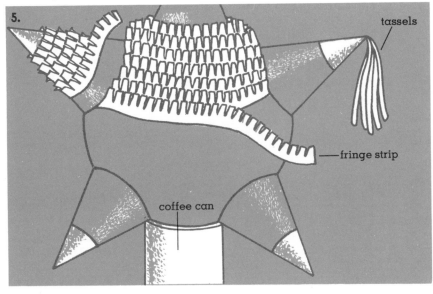

5.

tassels

fringe strip

coffee can

Posada songs

This Is the Night

74

Asking for a Lodging

Slowly (♩.=44)

(JOSEPH) O - pen these por - tals, I pray, for the love of heav - en.

O - pen your heart for a poor wom-an waits out - side.

Wea - ry from trav - el, we seek here a place to rest.

Please give us lodg - ing for my wife can

no long - er ride.

Let the Doors Be Open

Joyfully (♩=152)

mf En - ter pil - grims, let the doors be o - pen, let the doors be *mp*

o - pen; There is lodg - ing here with - in. You are wel - come in this hum - ble

dwell - ing, let there be re - joic - ing! Bless our house and en - ter in.

Friends Now Joyfully Gather

Moderately fast (♩=104)

mf Friends now joy - f'lly gath - er, kneel now ev - 'ry - one. Pay de - vot - ed

hom - age to the heav'n - ly Son, to Jo - seph and Mar - y, to th'ex - alt - ed Son.

Adoration

Smoothly flowing (♩ = 116)

p sempre legato

Come, all ye souls who love them. Come, see the ho-ly fam-'ly. Come, see the lit-tle man-ger. Kneel now and see them there.

E - ven the hum-ble don-key, Bends down his head in won-der.

Lambs with the shep-herd wor-ship, Bow down their heads in pray'r.

poco rit.

Index

Illustration acknowledgments

cover: Photo by Dean Jacobson
2: (left) Guillermo Aldana E.;
(right) *Artes de Mexico*
3: *Excelsior, Mexico*
6: World Book illustration
8: Franz Stoppelman
10: Pinacoteca Virreinal de San Diego,
Mexico City (Carlos Alcázar S.)
11: Biblioteca Nacional de Madrid
(*Artes de México*)
12-13: Pinacoteca Virreinal de San Diego, Mexico
City (Carlos Alcázar S.)
14: (top) Hospital Infantil, Mexico City
(*Artes de México*);
(bottom) Franciscan Convent,
Cuauhtinchan, Mexico (*Artes de México*)
15: Collection of Teresa Castelló de Yturbide
16: World Book photo by Joseph A. Erhardt
18: (top) Douglas Kirkland,
The Image Bank;
(bottom) *Kena*
19: (top) *Excelsior, Mexico;*
(center and bottom) *Kena*
21: *Artes de México*
22: (top) Douglas Kirkland,
The Image Bank
22-23: (bottom) Douglas Kirkland,
The Image Bank
24: Douglas Kirkland, The Image Bank
25: Wiltraud Zehnder
27: Douglas Kirkland, The Image Bank
28: Robert Schalkwijk
30: (top right) Robert Schalkwijk;
(center left) Franz Stoppelman
31: *Kena*
32-33: Roberto Aguilar M.
34: (top) Lilia Moreno de Maass;
(center) Guillermo Aldana E.;
(bottom) Roberto Aguilar M.
35: (top) Roberto Aguilar M;
(bottom) *Artes de México*

36: (top left) Robert Schalkwijk
36-37: (top) Roberto Aguilar M.
38: Douglas Kirkland, The Image Bank
40-41: (top) Roberto Aguilar M.;
(bottom) Wiltraud Zehnder
42: Ellen Kadelburg
43: Wiltraud Zehnder
44: Lilia Moreno de Maass
45: (left) Douglas Kirkland,
The Image Bank;
(right) Roberto Aguilar M.
46-47: (top) Robert Schalkwijk
46: (bottom right) Guillero Aldana E.
47: (bottom left) Douglas Kirkland,
The Image Bank
49: (upper left) Douglas Kirkland,
The Image Bank;
(lower left) Franz Stoppleman;
(right) Roberto Aguilar M.
50-53: Museo Nacional de Artes e Industrias
Populares
54: Roberto Aguilar M.
56: Roberto Aguilar M.
57: (left and right) Robert Schalkwijk
58: (top) Wiltraud Zehnder;
(bottom) Douglas Kirkland,
The Image Bank
59: (top left) Wiltraud Zehnder;
(top right) Roberto Aguilar M.
60-61: James P. Rowan
62-63: Bob Scott Studios, Inc.
65-73: John Walter and Associates